Cape Young

Wharekauri

Mairangi

Mt Chudleigh

L. Waikauia

Ta

Maunganui Beach

Tupuangi

Ngatikitiki

Tioriori

Waihi Crk

Tutuhi Crk

Maunganui

Waitangi West

Stony Crossing

PORT HUTT RD

Ohira Bay

Airpo

Te Roto

Tennants

Port Hutt

Whangatete Inlet

Lake

(Whangaroa Harbour)

L. Marakapia

Long Beach

Ocean Bay

Moreroa

Western Reef

PETRE BAY

Te

L

Red Bluff

Te One

Te Mata

Point Weeding

L.
(Huro)

Waitangi

Te Awatea

Wairarapa Crk

Te Awatea

OWENGA RD

Awarakau

Naiim R.

Ohinemama

Point Durham

TUKU RD

Awatotara Creek

Tuku-a-tamatea River

Point Gap

L. Rakeinui

L. Te Rangatapu

The Horns
Cape L'Eveque

Green Point

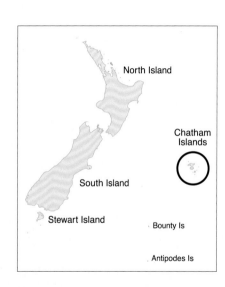

North Island

Chatham
Islands

South Island

Stewart Island

Bounty Is

Antipodes Is

AURI)

Kaingaroa

Point Munning

Te Whakaru Island

Koromaunga

Okawa Point

Hapupu

Waikeri Beach

e Kaingarahu

Makuku

airae

HANSON BAY

ki

FORTY FOURS
(MOTUHARA)

Owenga

Manukau Point

TRAIT

PITT ISLAND
(RANGIAURIA)

Flower Pot

bbit Island

Tupuangi

Hakepa

STAR KEYS
(MOTUHOPE)

ISLAND

Waihere
Bay

he Castle

North Head

Waipaua Stream

ngiauria Point

Glory Bay

Eastern Reef

Murumuru

RANGATIRA
(SOUTH EAST ISLAND)

THE PYRAMID
TARAKOIKOIA)

N

0   25 km

CHATHAM ISLANDS

Heritage and Conservation

CHATHAM ISLANDS

Heritage and Conservation

Edited by Colin Miskelly

CANTERBURY UNIVERSITY PRESS

in association with the
Department of Conservation

UNIVERSITY OF CANTERBURY
Te Whare Wānanga o Waitaha
CHRISTCHURCH NEW ZEALAND

First edition published in 1996
Reprinted 1999
Revised and enlarged edition published in 2008 by
CANTERBURY UNIVERSITY PRESS
University of Canterbury
Private Bag 4800, Christchurch
NEW ZEALAND

www.cup.canterbury.ac.nz

ISBN 978-1-877257-78-0

A catalogue record for this book is available from the
National Library of New Zealand

Copy-edited by Rachel Scott
Design and pre-press production by Mark Winstanley
Cover design by Mark Winstanley
Printed by Sunny Young Printing Ltd, Taiwan

Main cover image: Rangaika cliffs, southeast Chatham Island. *Colin Miskelly*
Insets left to right: Rakau momori (Moriori tree carving). *Ian Cooksley*; Red admiral butterfly on Chatham
Island forget-me-not. *Helen Gummer*; Black robin. *Don Merton*; Tarahinau tree at sunset. *Darren Scott*
Half-title page: Mangere and Little Mangere Islands, with Tarawhenua peninsula (Pitt Island) and
Rabbit Island in foreground. *Sharon Pirika*
Title page: Rangatira Island wave platform, with Hakepa hill, Pitt Island in the distance. *Graham Wood*
Contents page: Tarahinau tree at sunset. *Darren Scott*
Editor's acknowledgements: Chatham Island forget-me-not. *Sönke Hardersen*
Preface: Mustering at North Head, Pitt Island. *Peter Johnson*
Foreword: Chatham Island mollymawk in front of the Murumurus and Pitt Island,
with Mangere Island in the distance. *Tui De Roy*

CONTENTS

EDITOR'S ACKNOWLEDGEMENTS

In 1996 Allan Munn and his team of contributing authors and photographers produced a landmark publication on the Chatham Islands. That first edition of *Chatham Islands: Heritage and conservation* was a comprehensive and authoritative account of the islands' human and natural history. Twelve years on it provided a solid platform for the second edition. Several chapters had weathered well, and needed little updating. Others had been left behind by exponential growth in both knowledge and conservation effort. This revision has allowed the addition of two chapters ('Freshwater wetlands' and 'People who made a difference'), and text boxes covering species groups previously overlooked, including mosses, liverworts, lichens, fungi, spiders, land snails, freshwater fish and the endemic skink.

Nine of the original authors have again contributed (two post-humously), and there are six new chapter authors and eight text box authors. I thank them all for the quality of the material provided, and for their willingness to action editorial requests. I thank also Leah Fisher (daughter of Te Miria Wills-Johnson), and Jonathan and Rachael King for their support in the updating of their late parents' contributions.

Changes in printing technology meant that none of the original photographs were available via Canterbury University Press. I am extremely grateful to the original photographers for their willingness to dig out their transparencies, and to the many photographers who deluged me with additional digital images, prints and slides. The thousands of gorgeous images submitted would do justice to dozens of books. Thank you also to the many museum, library and research staff who assisted my quests for obscure images, particularly Max Barclay, Alison Harding and Sally Jennings (Natural History Museum, UK), Alexandra Caccamo (National Botanic Gardens, Glasnevin, Ireland), Helen Cohn (Royal Botanic Gardens, Melbourne), Malcolm Francis, Reyn Naylor and Steve Chiswell (National Institute of Water & Atmospheric Research, NZ), Jane Macknight, Eva Sullivan and Katie Wilson (Canterbury Museum, NZ), Caroline Thomas (Museum of New Zealand, Te Papa Tongarewa), and Petra Wollgast (Übersee-Museum, Bremen). All the photographs, paintings and maps were skilfully prepared for publication by Jeremy Rolfe, an artisan of his trade and valued adviser on content, grammar and aesthetics.

I acknowledge the institutional support from the Department of Conservation that allowed me to complete writing, editing and project management in a tight timeframe. Alan McKenzie, Jeff Flavell and Ken Hunt and their teams have assisted in innumerable ways. I am particularly grateful for the willing assistance provided by Amanda Baird, Joanna Haigh, Dave Houston, Ken Hunt and Alex McKillop, and by the Head Office librarians Janet Forbes, Shona Mackay and Ferne McKenzie. This revision was both sought and supported throughout by the Chatham Islands Conservation Board, especially Lois Croon and Peter Johnson.

Perceptive comment on individual chapters was provided by Brian Bell, Nadine Bott, Bill Carter, Alison Davis, Rhys Richards and Paul Scofield. The entire text benefited from careful scrutiny and comments provided by Amanda Baird, Dave Houston, Ken Hunt, Peter Johnson and Kate McAlpine. Kate also ably assisted with preparation of the index. Finally, I thank Rachel Scott (Canterbury University Press) and Mark Winstanley (Go Ahead Graphics) for the superb job they did of turning a pile of text and images into a beautiful book.

In closing, I wish to acknowledge contributors who are no longer with us: original authors Te Miria Wills-Johnson, David Given and Michael King, and Richard King of Canterbury University Press. Richard was closely involved in production of the first edition, and guided the first nine months of this revision. His premature death was a great loss to New Zealand publishing.

Me rongo
Colin Miskelly

PREFACE

The Chatham Islands Conservation Board was formed in 1990 to provide a link between the Department of Conservation and the Chatham Islands community. Since then, 31 Chatham Island and Pitt Island residents have served on the board, exposing many Chatham families to DOC and its work, and ensuring that a wide range of landowner perspectives were shared.

One of the first decisions made by the board was to work with DOC to produce a general interest book on the natural and cultural history of the islands. The first edition was published by Canterbury University Press and the Department of Conservation in 1996, and contained chapters by two board members. It served its purpose well, but 12 years on it is both out of print and out of date. The conservation gains during that time have been nothing short of spectacular, and this second edition is a timely update.

In 1996 there were 11 parcels of private land on the Chatham Islands, totalling 440 hectares, that were protected by conservation covenants. By early 2008 there were 40 parcels amounting to nearly 3000 hectares, indicating the huge commitment that Chatham Island and Pitt Island landowners have made to protecting their heritage. Concurrent with this land protection, much of the unique Chatham wildlife has responded well to conservation management, especially predator control. Examples include a threefold increase in Chatham Island oystercatchers to about 330 birds, and an 83 per cent increase in parea (Chatham Island pigeon) over the same period. In 1996, no taiko chicks fledged from known burrows, and only seven had survived over the previous five years. In 2008 there were 13 chicks, to add to the 46 others fledged since 2003.

Conservation Board members have been particularly pleased to participate in the efforts to restore wildlife to sites where they can be seen and appreciated by the community and their guests. In addition to the greater visibility of oystercatchers and parea, since 2002 there have been efforts made to restore black robin, Chatham petrel and Chatham Island snipe to a predator-fenced site on Pitt Island, and Chatham petrel and Chatham Island taiko to Sweetwater Conservation Covenant on the main island. Both these sites are on private land, with the predator-proof fence at the latter site funded through the efforts of the Chatham Island Taiko Trust. These projects are in their early stages, but show a welcome change from earlier perceptions that rare Chatham wildlife was locked up on outlying nature reserves, with access restricted to DOC staff and film crews.

While fishing and farming remain the mainstays of the Chatham Islands economy, tourism is growing rapidly, and is a source of employment for many islanders. Most visitors to the islands come to experience the unique lifestyle, to enjoy the wild landscapes and food, and especially to see the endemic plants and birds in their natural settings. This book is a celebration of the natural and historical resources of the islands, and is designed to be a source of information for both islanders and visitors alike.

Conservation on the Chatham Islands requires close cooperation and trust between landowners and the Department of Conservation. We are greatly encouraged by the progress that has been made during our time on the Conservation Board, and look forward to even greater gains in the future.

Chatham Islands Conservation Board
Liz Tuanui   Chair 1998–1999
Phil Seymour   Chair 1999–2004
Toni Gregory-Hunt   Chair 2004–2007
Peter Johnson   Chair 2007–2008

FOREWORD

The Chatham Islands are special: a part of New Zealand but utterly separate, with a character and culture entirely their own. The ecology is special too. These are the islands of the black robin, once the world's rarest bird but now thriving, thanks to the efforts and ingenuity of dedicated conservationists. They are home also to the taiko, the parea and beautiful parakeets; and to the akeake tree, the magnificent Chatham Island forget-me-not and other plants found nowhere else.

The islands' first inhabitants, the Moriori, lived in isolation for centuries in the place they called Rekohu (Misty Skies), before European 'discovery' in 1791. They knew nothing of the world beyond The Sisters and the Forty Fours, outer islands that today are home to 6500 pairs of royal albatrosses.

The Moriori grew nothing. Their diet consisted mainly of birds and fish, especially shellfish, and seals. They ate berries of the kopi tree, fernroot and even flax. Although there was no cultivation, there was conservation. Food-gathering areas were kept in reserve and looked after. Moriori took their food away from harvest sites: nothing was left near the water, because they believed it would drive the fish away. Vast heaps of shells found inland bear testimony to this care.

These people took what they needed and looked after the rest. When they hunted muttonbirds, they left the burrows intact so that other birds would return.

They believed they would offend Maru, one of their guardian atua, if they despoiled their foodstuffs. They looked after the wildlife because it was their livelihood.

For the past 200 years, though, the story has been one of plunder. First there was wholesale exploitation of whales and seals, so that now only small numbers of seals remain. Whalers also cleared the forests, once a luxuriant haven for unique birdlife, for firewood to melt blubber.

The landscape of our islands is beautiful but now barren. More recently we have had the plunder of crayfish and blue cod, paua and other shellfish. Humans have made fortunes, but stripped the islands of much of their riches. They have made their money and moved away.

The older generation, like myself, joined the plunder. We took fish; we never planted trees. Now we are anxious about what we will leave for our grandchildren.

Harvesting nature has been our bread and butter. Without it we cannot survive. Once, politicians thought the Chathams an expensive nuisance, and wished they could tow the islands away and sink them. They talked about resettling us. The fishing boom changed that. The islands' position considerably extends New Zealand's territorial waters into the richest fishing ground in the world.

But the rampant despoliation must end. We need a balanced management approach, just as the Moriori people of old had. I believe the involvement of the Department of Conservation is one of the most exciting things to have happened here. It gives the Chatham Islands a future.

The first step is understanding, and this book is an important part of that. It is a grand celebration of our natural wealth. I am sure it will inspire islanders to fresh love and respect for their home, and arm them with the knowledge they need to become guardians of their heritage. And I hope it will help mainland New Zealanders appreciate what a wonderful asset they have 650 kilometres from their coast.

The first edition of this book was proposed by the Chatham Islands Conservation Board, and publication was arranged by DOC and Canterbury University Press. This partnership has reformed 12 years later for a revised edition; all should be congratulated for their ongoing commitment to the Chatham Islands and their heritage.

Alfred 'Bunty' Preece
Owenga

INTRODUCTION

Most New Zealanders know of the Chatham Islands as the last place mentioned in their daily weather forecasts. Fewer may be aware that the islands, 800 kilometres east of Banks Peninsula and 45 minutes ahead in time, are the first part of the country to see the sun each morning.

The group of scattered islands that make up the Chathams lies between the southern latitudes of 43 and 45 degrees, in the path of the Roaring Forties. For much of the year the climate is temperate – maximum temperatures in the low twenties in midsummer, for example. In winter, however, mean temperatures drop to between 5–8°C. The lagoons and lakes on the main island and the vast expanse of ocean surrounding the group moderate the climatic extremes to which mainland New Zealand is subject.

Chatham, the largest island, has an area of around 92,000 hectares. It was known to the first inhabitants, Moriori, as Rekohu – 'Misty Skies' – on account of the mists that rise from the confluence of cold subantarctic currents meeting warm subtropical streams west of the group. Such mists often wreathe the islands for days at a time. The merging of waters also creates upwellings of nutrients that have attracted whales and seals and feeding birds to this part of the ocean in large numbers. Maori, who came later, called the island Wharekauri; a Royal Navy party led by Lieutenant William Broughton in the brig *Chatham* rediscovered Rekohu in November 1791 and gave the island its European name.

Almost a quarter of the inner surface of Chatham Island is covered

Top: Rainbow over Rangatira Island Nature Reserve. Graham Wood

An 1870s Moriori group dressed partly in traditional costume. From left: Te Ropiha, wearing a flax mat under a European shawl; Ropiha's wife, Uauroa, in a European blanket; Te Teira, maternal grandfather of Tommy Solomon (the last full-blooded Moriori), wearing a kura (parakeet feather head ornament), albatross feathers in his beard and a flax rain-cape, and holding a tupuari; and Pumipi, in a woven flax mat and also with albatross feathers in his beard.

Alfred Martin, Canterbury Museum, 19xx.2.314

by lagoons and lakes. The largest body of water is Te Whanga Lagoon, which dominates the eastern side and is intermittently open to the sea. Lake Huro nestles near the southwestern end of Te Whanga, and Lake Rangitai to the northeast. The perimeters of the large water bodies are beaded by lakelets.

Pitt Island, or Rangiauria, the second-largest island in the group and the only other one permanently inhabited, lies 17 kilometres to the south of Chatham. Its 6400 hectares of arable and lightly bushed land is higher and drier than most of the main island. The smaller and uninhabited members of the group include a number close to Pitt Island: Rangatira (South East) Island (249ha), now the major wildlife reserve for Chathams flora and fauna; Mangere Island (131ha); Little Mangere (Tapuaenuku); The Castle, and Sail Rock. Outlying islands include Star Keys (Motuhope); The Pyramid (Tarakoikoia), an important marker for 19th-century sailing vessels; the Forty Fours (Motuhara); and The Sisters (Rangitatahi). These last three are breeding grounds for large seabirds – albatrosses, mollymawks and giant petrels – whose fledglings Moriori, Maori and Pakeha Chatham Islanders traditionally harvested, along with sooty shearwater chicks (muttonbirds) from Mangere and Little Mangere Islands.

Pilot whale (blackfish) stranding, Te One, c.1910. Regarded by Moriori as gifts from the sea gods Tangaroa and Pou, stranded whales were often associated with human death.

W. B. Burt Collection, Alexander Turnbull Library, 038501

Moriori were the first human inhabitants of the islands, arriving at least 500 years ago. They came from the mainland of Aotearoa, and their ancestors were the same East Polynesian people who were ancestors of the Maori. Over the years of separation, however, each group evolved rather different cultures. Moriori developed their own dialect, discarded the distinctions between rangatira (chiefs) and commoners, and outlawed warfare and slavery. They were sufficiently different from the New Zealand Maori for each group to define themselves as separate peoples when they met in the 19th century. By the time of Broughton's visit the Moriori population on Chatham and Pitt Islands numbered about 2000.

Broughton's mapping of the north coast of Chatham Island and his report of large numbers of sea mammals in the vicinity brought sealers to the Chathams early in the 19th century. In 40 years they virtually wiped out the fur seal colonies on which Moriori had depended for food and clothing. They were followed in the 1830s and 1840s by whalers: first the ocean whalers, who replenished their food and water on the Chathams; and then the shore whalers, who based themselves at places such as Owenga, Te Whakaru, Okawa and Matarakau. Sealers and whalers introduced viral and bacterial infections, reducing the Moriori population to about 1600 by 1835. From the late 1820s some of these seamen were jumping ship and staying on the Chathams, becoming the islands' first European settlers.

Maori arrived in 1835. Two mainland tribes living at Port Nicholson, Ngati Mutunga and Ngati Tama, decided to relocate themselves to the

Whaling ships anchored off Waitangi, 1840. Painting by Charles Heaphy, draughtsman of the New Zealand Company.

Alexander Turnbull Library, B-043-014

Chathams. They seized the brig *Rodney* and forced its captain and crew to take them to the Chatham Islands in two shiploads. A total of 900 men, women and children were landed at Whangaroa (Port Hutt) in November and December. In the course of the next 12 months these new colonists 'walked the land' and killed about 300 Moriori, thus taking possession of the Chathams by right of raupatu, or conquest. The surviving Moriori were enslaved.

From this time on, Moriori numbers began to decline sharply as a result of further killings and demoralisation. By 1848 their population had been reduced to about 250, and it continued to decline throughout the 19th century.

The year 1840 brought further changes. The New Zealand Company sent representatives to buy the Chatham Islands from the Maori conquerors and settle larger numbers of Europeans there. One member of this expedition, the German naturalist Ernst Dieffenbach, became the first scientist to collect samples of Chathams flora and fauna, and the first to write about the plight of the Moriori. Money from the 'sale' of the islands enabled Chathams Maori to import horses and pigs, many of which escaped and, over a period of time, caused considerable damage to local flora.

The British government overruled the New Zealand Company

purchase, and in 1842 the Chathams were officially gazetted as part of New Zealand. That same year a group of five German Moravian missionaries arrived and settled on Chatham Island. They were followed by Methodist and Anglican missioners, who made converts but did not remain on the islands. Today most of the islanders are Anglican, and Anglican churches were built at Te One (St Augustine's) in 1885 and at Owenga (St Barnabas's) in 1928. Roman Catholics are the second-largest denomination, and their church, St Theresa's at Waitangi, dates from 1929. The Pentecostal, Methodist, Presbyterian, Ratana and Christian Fellowship churches have followers on Chatham Island, and the Mormons also visited and made converts.

Frederick Hunt and his family began farming on Pitt Island in 1843, and Maori exported potatoes to early settlers on the New Zealand mainland, and later to the Californian and Australian goldfields. Sheep farming began in 1841 and grew rapidly in the 1860s when Thomas Ritchie and Edward Chudleigh established stations at Kaingaroa and Wharekauri respectively. They leased or bought land from the Maori owners, and others soon followed their successful example.

For a period the islands' name was tarnished by the brutal behaviour of runaway seamen, and by fighting between Ngati Mutunga and Ngati Tama. The foundations of law and order were laid with the

Ngati Mutunga (left) and Ngati Tama fighting pa at Waitangi, 1840. Sketch by Charles Heaphy.

Alexander Turnbull Library, B-043-015-2

Fighting stages
Waitangi, Chatham I?
1839

C. Heaphy

appointment of the first Resident Magistrate, Archibald Shand, in 1855. He was followed in 1863 by the more effective Captain William Esdaile Thomas, who managed to persuade Maori to release the last of their Moriori slaves.

In the mid-1860s the New Zealand government, dealing with what

The first European house on the Chathams, built by German Moravian missionaries at Te Whakaru in 1844. It was owned by the Shand family when this photograph was taken in the 1890s.

Karl Gerstenkorn, Lovell-Smith Collection, Alexander Turnbull Library, 080786

Waitangi, 1868. Hauhau prisoners' huts at right; soldiers' redoubt overlooking the beach at left. The courthouse is on the beach with a flagpole in front and 'Te Kooti's gaol' behind.

Sketch by Stephenson Percy Smith, Alexander Turnbull Library, 020207

it considered to be Maori rebellion in parts of the North Island, decided to use the Chathams as a penal colony, and 300 Hauhau prisoners and their families, including the future Ringatu leader Te Kooti Arikirangi Te Turuki, were exiled there in 1866. They worked on farms and roads around Chatham Island until 1868, when Te Kooti led them in a successful breakout and escape back to New Zealand. The Native Land Court sat for the first time in the Chathams at Waitangi in 1870, and confirmed Maori ownership of the islands by right of conquest. The dwindling Moriori population (down to about 90 survivors by that year) was awarded half a dozen small reserves on which to subsist.

From the 1860s European settlers and some Maori wanted larger and more permanent dwellings and farm buildings. Suitable timber was scarce, however, and much of it had to be imported from the New Zealand mainland (kauri and totara) and from Australia. These homes and farms also required wood for cooking, laundering and heating. The combination of these needs and the demand for more pasture to graze sheep resulted in the felling and clearing of bush on Chatham, Pitt, Rangatira and Mangere Islands, with devastating consequences for the indigenous birds and insects. The introduction of cats, European rodents and possums contributed to the toll of extinctions. European

Waitangi, 2007.

Peter Johnson

settlers also brought blackberry, gorse and boxthorn for shelterbelts, and these seeded and spread rapidly.

The number of Moriori continued to decline; the last full-blooded Moriori, Tommy Solomon, died in 1933. Many of their descendants – Solomons, Preeces, Thompsons and Davises – continue to identify as Moriori, and so the original people of the Chathams retain a presence, along with Maori and Pakeha. Many residents trace descent from all three groups.

Like their New Zealand cousins, Chatham Island Maori were forbidden to speak their own tongue at school, and eventually knowledge of their traditional culture – their language, stories, songs and crafts – remained only with a few elderly women. In recent years, however, there has been a revival of this culture. A marae was established at Te One in the 1980s, and a kohanga reo soon afterwards.

Moriori culture, too, has undergone a renaissance. The magnificent Kopinga Marae was opened in January 2005; this enables visitors to experience the cultural and economic vitality of Moriori today.

Primary education has been available on the Chathams since the first school opened at Te One in 1885. There are now three primary schools: at Te One and Kaingaroa, and on Pitt Island. Secondary education remains a great expense for the islanders, however, with students obliged to travel to the mainland and board at the schools or with relatives. The New Zealand government provides a police officer, a courthouse, a hospital and a doctor. Local body responsibilities are carried out by the Chatham Islands Council, headed by a mayor; and the wharf, airport and electricity generation are administered by the Chatham Islands Enterprise Trust, composed largely of island representatives.

After the whaling and sealing eras, fish, especially blue cod, became the next Chatham resource to be exploited intensively, from 1910 until

Fishing boats at their moorings, Owenga, 1994.

Graham Wood

the mid-1950s. Many new settlers came to the islands during this period to work on the boats or in the associated fish factories. By the late 1960s a bonanza based on crayfish began, with a flotilla of boats descending on the islands. This five-year frenzy seriously depleted the resource. More recent years have seen a strong demand for paua, scallops and kina. Greater regulation of the fishing industry has protected stocks from the exploitation of earlier years, but Chatham Islanders are still resentful of the amount of fishing quota held by mainland-based fishers.

The 'us and them' attitude between Chatham Islanders and mainlanders dates from the 19th century and has been accentuated by what islanders regard as the indifferent treatment accorded them by successive governments and government departments. When anything needed to be done, islanders felt that the Chathams were always at the bottom of priority lists drawn up in Wellington. Some local sensitivities have also been offended by visitors who have returned to the mainland and appeared to denigrate Chatham Islanders in books, newspapers and official reports. Such local feeling is a strong positive force when it comes to islanders helping one another or dealing with emergencies such as ship strandings. A more positive outlook towards 'New Zealand' is being established as islanders make greater use of shipping and air-freighting links to export their fish and farming produce, and more tourists come to the islands.

Fishing and farming remain the economic backbone of Chatham Islands life, as they have done for over a century. Some farms are still worked by the descendants of the original owners. All this provides

Windswept akeake and farmland at Whangatete, Chatham Island.
Don Hadden

continuity for the 600 island residents at a time when the pace of change might otherwise distance them from their history and traditions.

The Chatham Islands retain an ethos of rural self-sufficiency now lost from most of mainland New Zealand. About 15 per cent of households cannot receive reticulated power, though the thumping of diesel generators is gradually being replaced by sustainable alternatives, including wind, solar and micro-hydro power. There is no cellphone coverage on the islands but according to the 2006 census, households with internet access (55 per cent) had almost equalled the number with a fax machine (58 per cent). And by 2007 about 73 per cent of households had satellite television installed, leading to the demise of the local television station, as islanders can access news and programmes from anywhere in the world.

As part of the determination to retain links with their past, most Chatham Islanders now accept that the destruction of plant and bird life must stop. Many landowners have agreed to fence off their remaining stands of bush and, where this has been done, forest regeneration has been astonishingly rapid.

Most New Zealanders know about the success of the campaign to save the black robin that began in the 1970s; fewer know that the parea, or Chatham Island pigeon, is again being seen in parts of Chatham Island where it has been absent for years. Families who have been dependent on nature for their livelihood for more than a century are at last learning the lesson that the first Chatham Islanders, the Moriori, knew well: that to rely on the bounty of nature it is necessary to live in harmony with the natural world.

Fenceposts destined for reserve and covenant fencing projects, Flower Pot, Pitt Island, 2002.

Peter Johnson

CHAPTER ONE

HUMAN SETTLEMENT AND HISTORIC SITES

The Chatham Islands have been occupied by humans for at least 500 years. In Moriori times the inhabited islands were Chatham, Pitt and, sporadically, Rangatira. The smaller islands – Mangere, Little Mangere, The Sisters, Forty Fours, Star Keys and The Pyramid – were visited seasonally for bird-harvesting and fishing. Chatham and Pitt Islands have been occupied continuously, and Rangatira and Mangere Islands were farmed intermittently until the 1960s, when they were gazetted as nature reserves.

Two factors have led to a wealth of evidence of human activity on Chatham and Pitt Islands. One is the relative density of the pre-European population, which in the 18th century numbered around 2000 people, about three times the current total population. By contrast, the density of people remained low in the 19th and 20th centuries, and there has been virtually no urban or industrial development on the islands. This has ensured that relics of the past – above and below ground – have survived rather better on the Chathams than they have in most parts of mainland New Zealand. This contributes to a feeling experienced by many visitors to the islands: that local history is close to them, and that the past and present on the Chatham Islands are connected more intimately than elsewhere.

The Maori cultural revival on mainland New Zealand in the 1970s and 1980s has been matched by a renaissance of Moriori and Maori

Top: **Mangoutu Hotel on Waitangi waterfront, c.1910.**
Ernest Guest, Guest Collection, Alexander Turnbull Library, 037617

House of Heta Namu and Paranihia Heta at Manukau Moriori settlement, 1890s. The house, built from horizontal ponga logs in a style known as wakawaka, is typical of post-contact Chatham Islands dwellings.

Karl Gerstenkorn, Lovell-Smith Collection, Alexander Turnbull Library, 080801

tikanga, values and language on the Chathams since the 1980s. This has led to wider appreciation of historic sites and relics. Many of the places of historical interest on the Chathams are on private property and may not be visited without the permission of the landowners. Owners' names are not listed here because such a list would become outdated as properties change hands. It is the responsibility of visitors to enquire locally to find out whom they should contact before they visit a particular site.

It should be noted that most of these sites are protected by the Historic Places Act and the Antiquities Act, which forbid any interference with structures or removal of artefacts. Fossicking for historical relics is not only unwelcome on the Chathams: it is illegal. If visitors do discover an artefact uncovered by the elements – perhaps an old bottle or a Moriori chisel – that they think needs to be 'rescued', they must hand it in to the Chatham Islands Council office in Waitangi for deposit in the museum.

Moriori sites

So far as we know, the discoverers of the Chatham Islands and first settlers there were Polynesian people who sailed from Aotearoa in or before the 16th century. They brought with them tools made of argillite and obsidian, and names for the region's plants, birds and fish. Over the following centuries, these people developed a culture that differed in many important respects from that of their relations on the mainland. The Chatham Island Polynesians outlawed warfare, they largely discarded notions of rank, they abandoned horticulture, and developed their own dialect. This was the culture and the people that came to be known as Moriori.

Most of the sites associated with the period of Moriori occupation of the Chathams take the form of parahanga (middens, or food rubbish dumps) and burial sites. Parahanga are usually discernible as heaps of shells appearing from eroding banks or sand dunes. They are found close to foraging or eating places, and the shells were discarded after the meat was scooped out of them, or after cooking (in which case they may be blackened and mixed with charcoal). Such dumps often include the bones of various birds, fish and sea mammals, which also formed a large part of the Moriori diet. They provide archaeologists, scholars and descendants with important evidence about the economies, diets and lifestyles of the islands' original inhabitants.

Some of the major Moriori sites that can be visited and viewed contain rakau momori (dendroglyphs, or tree carvings), and some caves contain hokairo manu (petroglyphs, or rock carvings).

Rakau momori were found formerly on kopi trees around the north, east and west coasts of Chatham Island, and also on Pitt Island. Most, however, were concentrated in kopi groves on the northeast coast of the main island. It is there that they can be viewed today, especially in J. M. Barker (Hapupu) National Historic Reserve, and Taia Bush Historic Reserve.

Most of the surviving rakau momori are stylised human figures of a kind often used in recent years as a Chatham Islands emblem. Others represented albatrosses and flounder, and some were more abstract. It is believed that the human figures represented known ancestors and were carved as acts of mourning and remembrance when kinfolk died.

The hokairo manu occur mainly in the limestone cliffs along the west side of Te Whanga Lagoon. These are predominantly carvings of stylised seals, and may have been associated with hunting rituals. Some appear to be stylised albatrosses, while others are not easily interpreted. The largest concentration of rock carvings can be seen at Te Ana a Nunuku (Nunuku's Cave; see page 42) on the lagoon shore at Moreroa. This site is associated with the ancestor Nunuku Whenua, who, according to tradition, outlawed group combat among Moriori clans. A comparison of the cave today with photographs taken in the late 1800s reveals that many of the seal carvings have been lost to the combined effect of wind, water and rubbing by stock. But those remaining still provide an impressive and moving glimpse of old Moriori material culture.

Human bones (koiwi) turn up in many parts of the Chathams, especially on eroding coastlines and in sand dunes. Unlike mainland Maori, Moriori tended not to use urupa, or graveyards; rather, the dead

Rakau momori at J. M. Barker (Hapupu) National Historic Reserve.

Peter Johnson

Moriori meeting house at Wairua, 1890s; Kiti Riwai and her daughter at right. This was the only Maori-style meeting house built in a Moriori community.

Preece Family Collection, Alexander Turnbull Library, 190171

were often buried sitting up to their necks in sand, facing out to sea. Such interments would eventually be covered over by the elements, exposed and then covered again in the succeeding years. Anyone coming upon signs of such a burial should simply leave it alone. Human bones should never be removed or touched by visitors.

Many places on Chatham Island have considerable significance for Moriori history and therefore for Moriori descendants. Wairua, on the northeast shore of Te Whanga Lagoon, is the site of one of the 1870 Moriori reserves and of a late 19th-century Moriori marae and meeting house. This is turangawaewae for the families descended from Riwai Te Ropiha and Tamihana Heta.

Te Awapatiki, south of the mouth of Te Whanga Lagoon, was the site of the major Moriori marae, where people from all tribes gathered to consider issues of island-wide significance. This was the place where Moriori discussed how best to deal with the Maori invasion of 1835, and it was the scene of a series of runanga meetings in the 1860s as Moriori drew up letters and petitions to the New Zealand government, set laws for their own communities, and debated how to preserve their culture in a rapidly changing world. In 1994 Moriori opened their claim to the Waitangi Tribunal at Te Awapatiki.

Manukau, on the southeast coast of Chatham Island, is a Moriori reserve, now owned by the Solomon family. Here stands a statue of Tommy Solomon, erected by his descendants and unveiled in 1986 as a memorial to all deceased Moriori. Further towards Manukau Point is a cemetery containing the graves of several Moriori families, including the Solomons and Preeces; and high on the hillside are the remains of the homestead built by Rangitapua Solomon in the early years of the 20th century and later the home of Tommy Solomon and his wife and four children.

Several places on Chatham Island were formerly Moriori stone workshops. The most important is a quarry on the coast adjacent to the basalt columns at Ohira, near Port Hutt (Whangaroa).

The modern Moriori marae at Te Awatea, overlooking Lake Huro and Te Whanga Lagoon, was opened by Prime Minister Helen Clark in January 2005. The marae's name, Kopinga, refers to the ancient gathering places of Moriori among the groves of kopi trees on the islands.

Left: Tommy Solomon statue at Manukau.
Richard Suggate, DOC

Right: Dignitaries arriving at the opening of Kopinga Marae, January 2005. From left: Hera Haunui (Tainui), Te Arikinui Dame Te Atairangikaahu (Maori Queen), Margaret Wilson (Attorney-General, and Minister in Charge of Treaty of Waitangi Negotiations), Helen Clark (Prime Minister), Annette King (MP for Rongotai, including the Chatham Islands), and Mahara Okeroa (MP for Te Tai Tonga, including the Chatham Islands).
Sharon Pirika/Hokotehi Moriori Trust

Maori sites

Because Maori residence in the Chatham Islands dates from the 1830s, there are fewer historic Maori sites. Whangaroa (Port Hutt) was where Ngati Tama and Ngati Mutunga recuperated from their voyage of colonisation in 1835, and where Pomare of Ngati Mutunga built the first Maori pa on the Chathams. No visible sign of that initial occupation remains.

Nor is there much evidence of early Maori days in Waitangi. The first Ngati Tama pa, later seized by Pomare and Ngati Mutunga, was on the east side of the Nairn River. Its centre lay where there is now a road construction depot. By the 1850s, in addition to houses, the pa had a large meeting house (on the present site of the fire-brigade headquarters) and a church. Both these community buildings were gone

This Maori meeting house was built at Waitangi in the 1880s and survived until 1927.

E. J. Moffat Collection, Canterbury Museum, 1960.41.6

by the late 1800s, but a second meeting house was built in the 1880s and survived until 1927. A Maori cemetery on the river side of the pa, where a pohutukawa tree stands today, was partly washed away by flooding and many of the remains were exhumed and buried elsewhere.

The so-called 'Te Kooti's gaol' stood alongside the Waitangi Hotel until 1979. Built by Maori convicts in 1867 from local sandstone, it was a relic of the days when Hauhau prisoners from the North Island were transported to the Chathams. Te Kooti Arikirangi Te Turuki, who founded his Ringatu religion on the Chathams before escaping with his fellow prisoners on the ship *Rifleman* in 1868, was never actually interned in the building.

Two houses belonging to the Daymond family, and their woolshed (built in 1882), are the oldest buildings of Maori significance that survive in Waitangi. Headstones of some of the 19th-century Ngati Mutunga chiefs, such as Wi Naera Pomare, father of Sir Maui Pomare, can be seen in Waitangi Cemetery, behind the racecourse.

In the 19th century, further major Maori settlements existed at Kaingaroa, Okawa, Matarakau, Wharekauri, Tupuangi and Mairangi. Few traces of these communities remain, other than the marked graves of the early Ngati Tama rangatira on Koromaunga Hill overlooking

Okawa, and a lone chimney from the kainga at Tupuangi, abandoned after a tsunami swept over the point in 1868. A Maori cave carving in the hill overlooking Mairangi has attracted much interest but is of recent origin.

Whakamaharatanga, the marae at Te One, is also recent. It is centred on the hall built in 1940 by a local farmer, Seaton Henderson, as a memorial to Chatham Islanders who had served overseas in the New Zealand armed forces and those who had lost their lives in boating accidents. The front of the hall has plaques commemorating those who died in the First and Second World Wars, and another listing the names of 11 men who drowned when the launch *Te Aroha* disappeared while travelling from Kaingaroa to Owenga in 1931.

So-called 'Te Kooti's gaol' at Waitangi.

Ron Scarlett Collection, Canterbury Museum, 3910

European colonial sites

The first European resident on the Chatham Islands was Jacob Tealing, who lived at Owenga from 1827 until his death in 1855. Others, also sealers like Tealing, were living at Te Whakaru and Ocean Bay by the early 1830s. They were joined by a handful of Maori, themselves attracted by the seal harvest, from Taranaki and Cook Strait.

The oldest European house in the Chatham Islands that is still inhabited is the former Hough cottage in Waitangi, behind the bottle store, near the Catholic Church. It is believed to date from around 1860, but no record has survived as to who built it, or for whom. The Hough family lived there from 1922 until the early 1970s.

The last of the grand Chatham Island homes of the 19th century is Nairn House, situated on the bank of the Nairn River near Waitangi. This was built of New Zealand kauri by William Baucke in two stages, in

Nairn House, the last of the grand 19th-century Chatham Island houses, built in the 1880s, photographed in 2007.

Peter Johnson

1882 and 1886. The first owner was Walter Hood, a merchant, runholder and shipowner until his bankruptcy in the 1890s. The house was owned by the Holmes family from 1925 until 1999.

Other buildings of historic interest in Waitangi include the general store, built as a hotel in Te One in the 1870s and shifted to Waitangi to double as a hotel and shop in 1905; St Theresa's Church, built in 1929; the Waitangi Hall, built to commemorate the New Zealand centenary in 1940; and Hotel Chathams, which, while it dates from only 1956, stands on the site of the old Mangoutu Hotel, built in 1866. At Whangamarino,

Travellers' Rest Hotel and general store, Waitangi, c. 1910.

Ernest Guest, Guest Collection, Alexander Turnbull Library, 013314

a few kilometres from Waitangi on the Owenga Road, the Preece family own and operate one of the oldest working woolsheds in the country, which was built for Arthur Cox and Alexander Shand in 1870.

The Waitangi Cemetery contains graves of many of the early Pakeha settlers, including Moriori and Maori scholar Alexander Shand (under one of the island's finest introduced pohutukawa trees) and Maria Baucke, a member of the German Moravian Mission. It also contains graves of several of Waitangi's early Maori leaders.

There are two important sites on the Ngaio coast south of Waitangi. The elegant homestead at Ohinemama was built by the former whaler Joe Santos in the late 1890s. Further down the coast, near Point Durham, are the remains of the powerhouse built for Mrs Santos in the 1930s as part of the island's first hydro-electric system.

Only one house in Owenga today, that owned by the Preece family, dates from the 19th century. Close by are the remains of Walter Hood's woolshed, built in the 1870s, and St Barnabas's Church, built in 1928. The cemetery on the seaward side of the church contains the graves of many early Owenga identities, including Apitea Punga and Jacob Tealing. Most of the graves are unmarked.

Mangoutu Hotel on Waitangi waterfront, c.1910.

Ernest Guest, Guest Collection, Alexander Turnbull Library, 037617

St Augustine's, built in 1885, is the oldest church on the Chatham Islands.

Dale Williams

The German Moravian Mission cottage at Maunganui, built in the 1860s using stone from the mountain behind.

Colin Miskelly

At Te One, north of Waitangi, the oldest house is that built in the 1880s by a former American whaler named Meikle. This is also the house in which Walter Hood and Johannes Engst, the last of the German missionaries, lived in their old age. St Augustine's Anglican Church (1885) is the oldest and the most beautiful church in the Chathams, and memorials on its walls and in its grounds remind visitors how many islanders have lost their lives through drowning. Te One's cemetery is the largest in the Chathams and includes the graves of many well-known settlers, including members of the Lanauze, Hunt, Fougere and Santos families, and that of Engst.

One of the most interesting houses remaining on Chatham Island is Maunganui cottage on the northwest coast, built by Johann Baucke and Johannes Engst between 1866 and 1868. This, the last outpost of the Moravian Mission, was constructed in local timber and stone and has withstood the years remarkably well.

The three grand 19th-century homesteads on the north coast – those of Edward Chudleigh at Wharekauri, the Grennell family at Matarakau, and Thomas Ritchie at Kaingaroa – are all gone. But a ponga shed built for Chudleigh by Hauhau prisoners in the late 1860s survives at Wharekauri – the last of a style of house that was common on the Chathams from the 1840s until the early 1900s.

There are two historic monuments at Kaingaroa. One, marked by a

whalers' trypot, commemorates those lost at sea off the northeast coast or drowned in the island's lagoons, and Tamakaroro, the Moriori killed by a British sailor on the adjacent beach in November 1791. (His name is wrongly recorded on the memorial as Torotoro.)

The second memorial, alongside the Kaingaroa Club rooms, was unveiled in 1991 to mark the bicentenary of the European discovery of the Chathams by William Broughton and his crew.

East of Kaingaroa, at Te Whakaru, are the remains of the first house built by the Moravian missionaries, using schist and mortar, in 1844. This was later acquired by the first Resident Magistrate, Archibald Shand, to accommodate his family of 12 children. Earlier, in 1840, a shore whaling station had stood for a short time on the same site.

Scattered relics of a larger whaling station, established by R. D. Hanson of the New Zealand Company in 1840, can be seen a little further south at Okawa: gigantic bones still protrude from the sand, whales' teeth are scoured out by the sea, and the remains of a schist-lined well survive in pasture a few metres inland from the beach. Other whaling stations, of which there are now no traces, were at Owenga and Matarakau and on Rangatira Island.

Some buildings associated with European colonial history of the

'Te Kooti's whare', built by Hauhau prisoners at Wharekauri. Ponga houses were common on the Chathams in the 19th century.
Colin Miskelly

Chathams survive on Pitt Island. These include the shepherd's cottage at Glory Bay built by William Jacobs in the late 1860s (see page 47), and the Bluff homestead built for William Hunt by William Baucke and William Jacobs in 1882. William Jacobs came to the Chatham Islands in 1866 to construct buildings for the Hauhau prisoners and their guards.

Other sites of interest are at Flower Pot, near the island's only wharf: the 19th-century gaol cell carved out of rock; and the memorial to Frederick and Mary Hunt, who raised their family on Pitt from 1843 and from whom many of the island's residents are descended.

Left: The 'Torotoro' memorial.
Right: The Bicentenary plaque. Both were erected at Kaingaroa on the northern coast of Chatham Island.

Don Hadden

CHAPTER TWO

GEOLOGY

The geology of the Chatham Islands will fascinate anyone interested in natural history. Few land areas in the world are so remote and can boast such geological diversity and such a prolonged history of volcanic activity confined to so small an area. Intriguingly, the Chatham Islands have existed as land only for about 2.5 million years, yet they have a subdued relief, reminiscent of the old, worn interior of a continent. The geology of the Chatham Islands tells us that their flat appearance relates to their comparatively recent emergence from the sea.

The fossil record of mid-Cretaceous (100–90 million years ago or Ma), Late Cretaceous (85–65 Ma), Paleocene to Eocene (63–34 Ma), and Miocene to Pliocene time (6–2.4 Ma) is particularly rich and important scientifically. However, the record for the past 34 million years generally is patchy and thin. These younger rocks are dominated by formations of coloured submarine volcanic ash known as tuff (e.g. Kahuitara Tuff, Red Bluff Tuff, Whenuataru Tuff, Momoe-a-Toa Tuff), and open-ocean sediments. The latter largely comprise biogenic ('sourced from animals') carbonate (Te Whanga Limestone, Onoua Limestone), and authigenic minerals such as greensand-forming glauconite (e.g. Tutuiri Greensand) and phosphorite-forming fluorapatite (e.g. Takatika Grit), which grow spontaneously from sea water within the sediments on the sea floor.

These interesting sedimentary rocks have survived subsequent

Top: Little Mangere Island from Mangere Island (foreground and to left), with The Castle in the distance. Helen Gummer

erosion largely as a result of their burial beneath volcanic rocks that erupted from small submarine volcanoes comparable in size to those preserved around Auckland city.

The Chatham Islands are also of particular geological interest because they provide a 'window' on the Chatham Rise. The only emergent fragment of this major submarine extension of the New Zealand subcontinent (Zealandia), these islands stand proud of it partly because they have been the site of repeated episodes of volcanic eruption over the past 85 million years, and partly because of tectonic uplift. Young submarine volcanic rocks, about 4 million years old, form the highest land surface (about 300 metres above sea level) in southwest Chatham Island. This is clear evidence that the Chatham Islands became emergent as land no earlier than that.

These oceanic islands are geologically remarkable in many respects, not least because metamorphic basement rocks (greywacke and schist) are exposed, revealing their true continental affinity, but also because

The oldest rocks in the Chathams include this Chatham Schist exposed at Te Whakaru Island, northeast Chatham Island.

Colin Miskelly

the overlying sedimentary rocks contain fossils that are not known from mainland New Zealand or anywhere else in the world. Furthermore, some of these rocks represent moments of geological time not represented in mainland New Zealand.

The geological history of the Chatham Islands is closely linked with that of mainland New Zealand, and can be described in terms of Gondwanaland (up until 83 Ma), Zealandia (83–23 Ma) and New Zealand (23 Ma to the present day).

The oldest rocks

Unlike most small island groups around the Pacific, the Chathams contain very old exposed continental rocks. They form the basement to all the younger (Cretaceous and Cenozoic) rocks and sediments known from the Chatham Islands and Chatham Rise. These are metamorphic rocks referred to as Chatham Schist, similar in composition, age and history to the greywacke and schist rocks of Otago and Canterbury in the South Island.

Metamorphic rocks, such as schist, are produced from pre-existing rocks deep within the earth by great pressures and high temperatures. Under these conditions the minerals recrystallise into new minerals that bear little resemblance to those of the original marine sediments and volcanic rocks from which they formed. However, parts of the Chatham Schist are less metamorphosed than others, such as at Matarakau, where original sedimentary bedding can be observed in places within sandstone formations better described as greywacke rather than schist.

Chatham Schist, with a minimum age of metamorphism of 160 million years, is the oldest rock exposed in the islands. It is restricted in outcrop to northern Chatham Island. The Forty Fours, rarely visited but representing the easternmost fragments of New Zealand, are also Chatham Schist. This island group is sometimes visible from the air on flights between Auckland and South America, the only international flights to cross the Chathams.

The original sediments (largely derived from granites and volcanic rocks) that form the bulk of these metamorphic basement rocks are of Permian to Triassic age (300–200 Ma). The source of the sediments was either the Queensland or western Antarctic segments of the ancient Gondwanaland supercontinent.

Plate tectonic setting

The Chatham Islands are on the Pacific Plate and lie almost 1000 kilometres east of the current boundary with the Australian Plate. The Alpine Fault, running in a northeast–southwest direction along the western margin of the Southern Alps, and its northern extension the Hope Fault, both in the South Island, define this boundary.

1868	Tsunami		
1835	Arrival of Maori		
1791	Arrival of Europeans		
AD 1500	Arrival of Moriori		
6500 BP	Sea level attains present position		
20,000	Last ice age; sea level 130 metres below present		
26,500	Oruanui Eruption of Taupo caldera, central North Island		
340,000	Rangitawa Eruption, central North Island		
350,000	Peat begins to accumulate		
1.8 Ma	Beginning of ice ages (Pleistocene time)		
2.4–1.8 Ma	The oldest sands accumulate (Titirangi Sand)		
3–2 Ma	Chatham Islands become emergent		
4–3 Ma	Submergence of Mangere volcano		
	Accumulation of limestone (Motarata Limestone)		NEW ZEALAND 23 Ma to present day
5–3 Ma	Widespread submarine eruption (Rangitihi Volcanics)		
	Rangatira	Mt Dieffenbach	
	Star Keys	Tawirikoko	
	The Horns	Middle Knob	
	The Sisters	Hokopoi	
	The Pyramid	Saddle hill	
	Mairangi	Ngatikitiki	
	Hikurangi	Motuporoporo	
	Cape Young	Ngapukemahanga	
	Maunganui	Motuariki	
	Matakitaki	Korako	
6–4 Ma	Formation of a crater lake on Mangere Volcano (Mangere Formation)		
6 Ma	Eruption of Mangere volcano and appearance of an island		
	Mangere	Sail Rock	
	Little Mangere	Waihere hill	
	The Castle	Rangiauria Point	
24–22 Ma	Accumulation of limestone (Taoroa Limestone)		
34–33 Ma	Australia and Antarctica part company; formation of circum-Antarctic current		
55–30 Ma	Accumulation of limestone (Te Whanga Limestone)		
	Widespread submarine eruption (Red Bluff Tuff; may have formed an island)		
	Red Bluff	Rangitihi	
	Te Awatea	Taupeka	
	Tikitiki Hill	Mt Chudleigh	ZEALANDIA 83–23 Ma
62–55 Ma	Accumulation of greensands (Tutuiri Greensand)		
63–62 Ma	Accumulation of phosphorite nodules (Takatika Grit)		
65 Ma	Cretaceous–Cenozoic boundary event: meteorite impact; global extinctions of the dinosaurs, marine reptiles, flying reptiles and ammonites		
70–65 Ma	Submergence of Chatham Volcano		
80–70 Ma	Accumulation of shallow water sands (Kahuitara Tuff)		
83 Ma	Zealandia rifts away from Gondwanaland		
	Formation of Tasman Sea and sea floor		
85–80 Ma	Eruption of Chatham Volcano (Southern Volcanics)		
	Main southern mass of Chatham	Waitaha Creek	
	Hakepa hill	Stony Crossing (basalt columns)	GONDWANALAND pre 83 Ma
100–90 Ma	Accumulation of deltaic, river and lake sediments (Tupuangi Formation; oldest sediments in the Chathams; restricted to Pitt Island and Mangere Island)		
190–170 Ma	Metamorphism of Chatham Schist		
290–220 Ma	Accumulation of original sediments that make up Chatham Schist; oldest rocks in the Chathams: the basement		

Palaeomagnetic studies of volcanic rocks indicate that the Chatham Islands, and hence the Chatham Rise, have maintained their present position in relation to the east coast of the South Island for at least 75 million years.

In terms of their tectonic setting, the volcanic rocks in the Chathams erupted well away from any plate margin, and so are quite different in character from volcanic rocks produced at the margin of a plate, such as those in the central North Island of New Zealand. This is borne out by the chemistry of Chathams volcanic rocks: they are the product of dry, high-temperature melting processes within the mantle, and are markedly different in character from the wet, explosive volcanic eruptions evident in the Taupo Volcanic Zone of the central North Island, including Ruapehu, Ngauruhoe and Tongariro.

The southern main mass of Chatham Island and northern Pitt Island are the remnants of a large Late Cretaceous (85–75 Ma) shield volcano. This relatively flat-lying volcano, now much eroded, was centred in the modern Pitt Strait. The spectacular sheer cliffs rising 100–250 metres above sea level along the almost inaccessible southern coast of Chatham Island expose a pile of gently northward-dipping basalt lava flows with inter-bedded volcanic rubble, scoria and ash deposits. Most of the lava flows are a type of basalt called hawaiite. Other rock types include trachyte and trachyandesite. Hakepa hill on Pitt Island is entirely composed of trachyte. Intrusive dyke rocks of pale-coloured trachyandesite are visible on the coast of Chatham between Point Weeding and Point Durham.

This pile of lava flows (Southern Volcanics Formation) and associated sedimentary deposits defines a surprisingly well-preserved sector

Opposite: A summary of major events in the long geological history of the Chatham Islands. The geological origins of the Chathams are expressed in terms of their Gondwanaland (pre-83 million years ago), Zealandia (83–23 Ma), and New Zealand (23–0 Ma) ancestry and heritage. Apart from the four most recent events, dates are given as Before Present (BP); Ma = million years ago.

Basalt columns (cooling structures) at Ohira Bay, northern Chatham Island. These lava flows (Southern Volcanics) erupted on land 85–80 million years ago.

Darren Scott

of the flank of a large, broad shield volcano, not unlike Hawaii. It has probably been stripped of any Cretaceous–Cenozoic cover sediments by Pliocene–Pleistocene marine erosion associated with uplift of the Chathams within the past 4 million years.

The steep cliffs and linear coastlines of southern Chatham are almost certainly controlled by faults, but none is visible and hence none has been mapped. If present, any faults must lie seaward of the present coastline, and obscure the more circular shape of the original volcano.

Exposures of Southern Volcanics can be seen in northern Chatham at Ohira Bay (Stony Crossing), where spectacular columnar-jointed lava flows of olivine basalt are exposed on the coast, and at Waitaha Creek.

The fossil record

The oldest fossil-bearing rocks in the Chathams can be seen on northern Pitt Island in the Tupuangi Formation of mid-Cretaceous age (100–90 Ma). They are largely river and estuarine sediments, and include some layers of lignite (coal). They contain abundant fossil spores of mosses and ferns, and pollen of conifers (including the ancestors of modern podocarps such as totara and rimu), and early flowering plants such as beeches. They also contain fossil wood, some silicified (petrified) and some carbonised.

These rocks are of considerable geological interest because they indicate that the Chathams were part of a continental landmass (Gondwanaland) 100–90 million years ago. At that time, the Chatham Rise must have been largely dry land. These old sediments represent the uplifted and eroded sediment fill of a valley or depression (half-graben)

The oldest sediments in the Chatham Islands (Tupuangi Formation), exposed in Waihere Bay, northern Pitt Island, contain fossils that are 100–90 million years old (mid-Cretaceous).

Hamish Campbell

that formed next to a major fault. This faulting is a widespread feature of the Chatham Rise, which formed during stretching of the crust in mid-Cretaceous time, prior to formation of the Tasman Sea floor, and gradual separation of Zealandia from Gondwanaland.

Also on Pitt Island, younger sedimentary rocks of Late Cretaceous age (85–65 Ma) can be seen on the coast at Kahuitara Point, immediately south of the wharf in Flower Pot Bay (Onoua), and in the cliffs on the south side of Tarawhenua peninsula. The original sediments were derived from volcanic rocks and deposited as sands in a shallow sea close to a beach. These rocks (Kahuitara Tuff) contain the oldest marine fossils known from the Chathams, including ancient squid-like animals called belemnites and ammonites. These are very similar to mainland New Zealand examples of the same age.

On Chatham Island the oldest fossil-bearing formation is the Takatika Grit, more than 45 million years younger than the oldest sediments exposed on Pitt Island (Tupuangi Formation). These rocks are of early Cenozoic age or, more specifically, the later part of the Early Paleocene age (63–62 Ma). They are represented by a thin sequence (about six metres) of marine greensands (glauconite- and phosphorite-bearing, with fossil bones) that are exposed only on northern Chatham, particularly along the Tioriori coast between Ngatikitiki and Tutuiri Creeks. This formation has attracted international interest in recent years because of the discovery of dinosaur fossils, along with bird and marine reptile fossils, by Jeffrey Stilwell and colleagues from Monash University, Australia. The Takatika Grit constitutes only the third known dinosaur locality within New Zealand. Because the dinosaurs and marine reptiles became extinct 65 million years ago, it is assumed that these fossils were probably 'reworked' from an older rock formation (about 75 million years old). Furthermore, dinosaurs are strictly terrestrial, yet the Takatika Grit accumulated on the sea floor at a water depth of several hundred metres. The bird fossils are of marine species, and may have been contemporary with Takatika Grit formation.

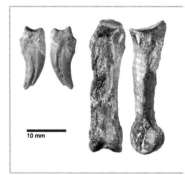

Two dinosaur bones extracted from rocks (Takatika Grit) exposed at Tioriori, northern Chatham Island. Life size.

Jeffrey Stilwell

These Takatika sediments post-date the eruption of the Southern Volcanics shield volcano to the south and were formed in the open ocean, well away from a continental landmass, in water depths of 200–400 metres. This means the land bridge that existed between the Chathams and mainland New Zealand 100–85 million years ago must have been completely severed by the time the Takatika Grit was deposited: the Chatham Rise had submerged and the Chathams had become isolated oceanic islands.

The Chathams have remained isolated throughout Cenozoic time (65 Ma to the present day), as reflected in the fossil and sedimentary record. This is dominated by limestone deposits that are characteristic of open-ocean conditions. The most widespread and conspicuous

The western shore of Te Whanga Lagoon, looking south from Motuhou Point towards Moreroa. The limestone cliffs (Te Whanga Limestone) are 56–33 million years old (Paleocene to earliest Oligocene age).

Hamish Campbell

limestones are of Late Paleocene to Early Oligocene age (56–33 Ma). A number of distinct limestones are recognisable on the basis of composition, fossil content and age.

The most widespread limestone formation on Chatham Island is found around the western shores of Te Whanga Lagoon. As with all limestones in the Chathams, this is almost entirely formed from the skeletal hard parts of marine organisms, in particular bryozoans (moss animals or lace corals) and plankton (foraminifera). These are too tiny to see easily, but more conspicuous are shelly fossils of sea urchins, barnacles, molluscs, brachiopods, and also shark teeth (for example at Blind Jims Creek). However, numerous other marine invertebrate and vertebrate fossils (whale bones) are preserved as well.

The petroglyphs preserved in cliffs on the western shore of Te Whanga Lagoon, at Moreroa near Motuhou Point, are carved into the

Moriori hokairo manu carved into Te Whanga Limestone between Motuhou Point and Moreroa, on the western shore of Te Whanga Lagoon.

Peter Moore

lowest strata of the Te One Limestone Member of Te Whanga Limestone. The limestone here is composed mainly of bryozoans and is about 36–37 million years old.

The more recent volcanic record

Associated with Te Whanga Limestone is Red Bluff Tuff, a relatively widespread sedimentary formation of volcanic origin and basalt composition. The original sediments largely comprised scoria and ash deposits that accumulated in a submarine environment in water depths of 100–400 metres. Tuff is consolidated volcanic ash, and scoria is volcanic explosion debris that accumulates near the crater and is highly vesicular (charged with gas bubbles). Red Bluff Tuff is a distinctive red-brown colour and is present in central Chatham Island as well as on Pitt Island. In places it is rich in fossils. It is the product of submarine volcanic activity that was probably sporadic but widespread during Early Paleocene to Early Eocene time (63–55 Ma). The age is determined from identification of fossil plankton (foraminifera and dinoflagellates) and mollusc shells. These fossils are particularly significant, as they represent faunas and marine environments of early Cenozoic age that are not known from elsewhere in the Southern Hemisphere.

Red Bluff Tuff is best seen in coastal exposures at Red Bluff, in the cliffs around Waitangi Harbour and the hills west of Waitangi (Point Weeding area and south), and on Pitt Island north of Flower Pot Bay, at Waihere Bay and Tarawhenua peninsula.

Spectacular layering within a pile of volcanic ash (Red Bluff Tuff) that accumulated on the sea floor 63–55 million years ago at Point Weeding, west of Waitangi. Red Bluff itself is the central feature in the distance.

Hamish Campbell

Rock-dating evidence suggests that there was some volcanism 42–34 million years ago during Eocene time. These rocks (Northern Volcanics) may have contributed to basaltic submarine ash deposits (Red Bluff Tuff), and are restricted in distribution, limited to Rangitihi hill, Mt Chudleigh, and the coast north of Mt Chudleigh and Taupeka Point. It is conceivable that Mt Chudleigh may have formed a small island in Middle to Late Eocene time, only to be subsequently eroded and submerged.

Two much younger eruptive centres are present in northern Chatham. These form the prominent landmarks of Maunganui and Cape Young. They are Pliocene in age (5 Ma) and date from a widespread episode of latest Miocene to Pliocene volcanic activity, 6–2.7 million years ago, that also produced The Sisters, Mangere Island and associated islets, Waihere hill, Rangiauria Point, the islets at the southern end of Pitt Island, Rangatira (South East) Island, Star Keys, and The Pyramid.

Mangere, Little Mangere, The Castle, Sail Rock and surrounding islets, along with Waihere hill and Rangiauria Point on Pitt Island, are the eroded remains of the crater, rim and satellite vents of a large volcano. In the central part of Mangere is a well-developed sequence of freshwater lake sediments (Mangere Formation) that accumulated in a crater lake, and so Mangere volcano must have risen above sea level and formed an island at the time of eruption, 6 million years ago. However, the island subsequently sank and was planed off by marine processes.

Rangatira Island is composed entirely of a dipping sequence of coarse-grained volcanic sediments that must have accumulated near

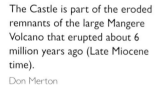

The Castle is part of the eroded remnants of the large Mangere Volcano that erupted about 6 million years ago (Late Miocene time).

Don Merton

Mts Dieffenbach, Hokopoi and Motuporoporo are small basalt volcanic cones (part of the Rangitihi Volcanics) on northern Chatham Island, which all erupted as submarine volcanoes when the Chathams were still totally submerged 5–4 million years ago (Early Pliocene time).

Colin Miskelly

a volcanic vent. However, these rocks are quite distinct from those associated with the Mangere volcano and were erupted later, about 4 million years ago.

There is increasing observational and dating evidence to suggest that many of the following northern Chatham Island volcanic centres, all still conical in form, erupted at about the same time as Rangatira Island, 5–4 million years ago: Korako, Motuporoporo, Motuariki, Ngapukemahanga, Waikauia, Hikurangi, Hokopoi, Mt Dieffenbach, Saddle hill, Tawirikoko and Matakitaki.

The Horns at Cape L'Eveque, in the southwest corner of Chatham Island, are the remains of volcanic pipes or throats that also erupted 5–4 million years ago. Associated lava flows and fossil-bearing volcanic tuff and limestone nearby form the highest topographic surface in the Chatham Islands. There is ample evidence of eruption and accumulation of sediments in a submarine environment. Clearly, the Chatham Islands were completely underwater at this time.

The dramatic peaks of The Horns, near Cape L'Eveque, southwest Chatham Island, are the remains of a volcano that erupted 5–4 million years ago (Early Pliocene) when the Chathams were still totally submerged. These young volcanic deposits are resting on much older cliff-forming basalt lava flows (Southern Volcanics).

John Begg

Some of the volcanoes referred to above have well-developed volcanic tuff sequences associated with them, and some of these sediments accumulated in shallow seawater environments, less than 200 metres deep. We know this from the presence of shallow-water fossils. The 5 million-year-old Cape Young eruption produced a distinctive formation called the Momoe-a-Toa Tuff, which contains some exquisitely preserved shell beds dominated by scallops and brachiopods (lamp shells) of earliest Pliocene age (c.5 Ma). These are restricted in distribution to Momoe-a-Toa Point, south of Cape Young. However, on the basis of other physical volcanological criteria, it is likely that most of these submarine volcanoes (listed above) erupted in deeper water of 200–400 metres depth.

On Pitt Island another distinctive formation (Whenuataru Tuff) also contains an extremely rich and diverse marine fauna. This is also of Pliocene age, and is best exposed at Motutapu Point at the northern tip of Pitt Island. It is widespread in the coastal sections around Flower Pot Bay and Tarawhenua peninsula, and undoubtedly is derived from eruptions of the Mangere volcano.

A spectacular shell bed of fossil scallops preserved in volcanic ash (Momoe-a-Toa Tuff) that erupted onto the sea floor 5–4 million years ago (Early Pliocene), exposed at Momoe-a-Toa Point, south of Cape Young, northern Chatham Island.

Colin Miskelly

Associated with Whenuataru Tuff is the Onoua Limestone, almost pure calcium carbonate, that is exposed in and around Flower Pot Bay and is notable for fossil brachiopods.

Peatlands

The most enduring impression of the Chathams landscape, particularly of Chatham Island, is the subdued, low-lying gentle topography, punctuated by the distinctive conical volcanic hills of northern Chatham. This is the result of a prolonged history of marine submergence, with emergence due to tectonic uplift through Late Pliocene to Recent time (3.6 Ma to the present). Surfaces cut by the sea are plainly evident as flat features on most of the islands but especially Rangatira Island, Pitt Island, The Sisters, Forty Fours and Chatham Island. A cover of sand is also widespread, but most conspicuous of all is the peat that has developed during Pleistocene time (the past 1.8 million years), but mostly since the last interglacial (about 100,000 years ago), and in particular since the last glaciation, which ended about 14,000 years ago.

There is evidence from interbedded volcanic ash beds such as the Rangitawa Tephra (about 340,000 years old) and the much younger Oruanui Tephra or Rekohu Ash (26,500 years old) that the peat started to accumulate at least 350,000 years ago and is still building up. It blankets the landscape in a layer up to 6 metres thick in places, and is largely responsible for the unique geological character of the Chathams. It indicates prevailing wet, cool conditions and poor drainage. Its characteristic vegetation is dominated by tarahinau (*Dracophyllum arboreum*) and bamboo-rush (*Sporadanthus traversi*).

Below and within the peat are tephras (beds of volcanic ash) that originated from huge rhyolite caldera eruptions located in the Taupo Volcanic Zone of the central North Island. The thickest known layer (Rangitawa Tephra) is more than 30 centimetres thick and was erupted more than 330,000 years ago. This is best observed in cliffs at the northern end of Red Bluff. The most widespread tephra, up to 16 centimetres thick, dates from a major eruption of the Taupo caldera known as the Oruanui event, about 26,500 years ago. It is widely observed in road cuttings on Chatham Island as a prominent pale layer sandwiched within the peat.

Historic Glory Cottage, Pitt Island, with Rangatira (South East) Island in the distance. Rangatira is composed entirely of volcanic debris erupted from a submarine volcano about 4 million years ago (Early Pliocene). A flight of planar marine-cut surfaces clearly visible on the island is evidence of a series of tectonic uplifts all within the past 4 million years.

Allan Jones

A profile of peat exposed near Maunganui Beach, northern Chatham Island, with conspicuous layers of pale volcanic ash. The uppermost band is Oruanui Tephra (or Rekohu Ash) that was erupted from Taupo, central North Island, 26,500 years ago.

Peter Johnson

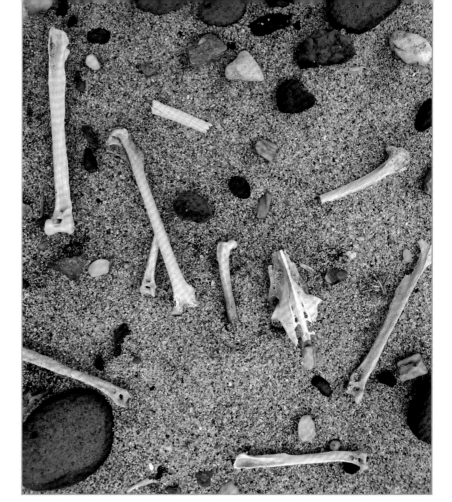

Subfossil seabird bones exposed on a dune slope at Ohira Bay. Prominent are bones of the extinct Chatham Island crested penguin (top left), Chatham Island taiko (on diagonal, centre left), Chatham Island blue penguin (lower left and bottom right), and Pitt Island shag (the pelvis and the diagonal bone to the right).

Colin Miskelly

Subfossil bird bones are commonly encountered in coastal areas of the Chatham Islands, especially in eroding sand dunes that are probably no more than 10,000 years old. Some layers are so rich in bone material that the sand has acquired a purplish-grey colour indicative of high phosphate content. Most of the bones relate to burrowing marine birds (petrels, prions and shearwaters).

A number of caves occur within Te Whanga Limestone along the western shore of Te Whanga Lagoon. Several have been excavated by palaeoecologists for bird bones. These sites have produced thousands of bones and are the primary basis of our knowledge of extinct birds of the Chatham Islands.

The dynamic modern landscape

The modern landscape features of Chatham Island – including Lake Huro, Te Whanga Lagoon, the many small lakes, extensive sand dunes and long sandy beaches – result largely from the prevailing westerly weather. The coast, especially the sandy beaches backed by sand dunes, is a mobile, rapidly changing landscape with low relief and readily eroded sediments underpinned in many places by relatively soft sedimentary rock.

Geologically, Te Whanga Lagoon is normally land-locked and is a lake filled with sea water diluted by the Te Awainanga River, which drains much of the extensive southern uplands of Chatham Island. When the lagoon entrance is open it becomes a temporary tidally influenced extension of the sea. Otherwise, the fluctuations of Te Whanga are driven primarily by the alternating of the predominant southwest wind with those from the north or northeast, causing the water level to be higher at one or other end, often for several days at a time.

Erosion of the western shore of Te Whanga Lagoon produces sediment that is transferred to the eastern shore, which is growing in land area. This is resulting in a smaller, shrinking lagoon, evident in aerial photographs of Chatham Island, which show broad bands of sediment on the floor of the lagoon that will be added to the eastern shore. Te Whanga may become more constricted and lake-like in character as time passes. However, with rising sea levels (3 centimetres in the past decade), perhaps it will become less lake-like.

Other sites within the Chathams group are also susceptible to weather-driven erosion, including coastal erosion, cliff collapse due to undercutting by the sea, and landslides, particularly along the south coast of Chatham and at Waihere Bay on Pitt Island.

In places, rich shell beds are preserved within the Pliocene–Recent sediments of central and northern Chatham Island. These represent fossil-beach accumulations. The finest examples are found within the Titirangi Sand Formation of Late Pliocene age (2.4–1.8 Ma) and exposed at Titirangi Point and Moutapu Point on Karewa Peninsula, northern Te Whanga Lagoon. There are many different species, and the shells are abundant, though not as plentiful as the Pliocene shell beds of the Whenuataru Tuff on Pitt Island.

Sandbars on the eastern side of Te Whanga Lagoon, with Taia Farm Historic Reserve beyond. These have formed within the past 10,000 years (Holocene), and are actively growing to produce new land as sediment is eroded from the western side of Te Whanga Lagoon and transported across it to the east.

Peter Johnson

There are significant differences from mainland New Zealand faunas of the same age: for example, no shells belonging to the ostrich-foot family (Struthiolariidae) occur at the Chathams, but these are common around the mainland. These faunas also suggest that the Chathams have been situated at the convergence of cool-water ocean currents (from the south) and warmer-water currents (from the north) since at least the Pliocene (5 Ma).

Younger Pleistocene and Holocene shell beds (1.2 Ma to the present day) are exposed near Waitangi and Owenga, and along the shores on the main beaches. Some of these may be confused with middens that are also common in these areas, but usually contain artefacts.

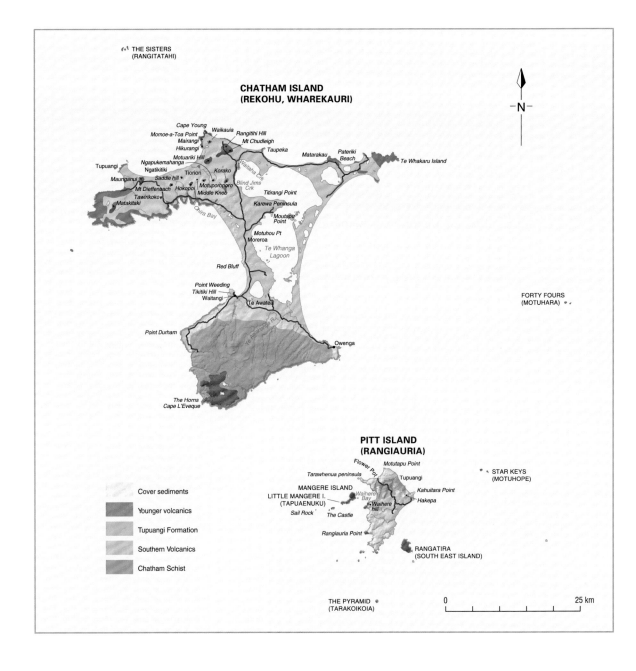

There is little of obvious economic value in the geology of the Chathams, and only the peat has received thorough appraisal. However, investigations during the 1970s and 1980s into the viability of extracting montan wax from peat concluded that it would be uneconomic and of high environmental impact. Montan wax is a heavy paraffin used in cosmetics, paint and other industries.

No precious stones are known from the Chathams. So-called 'Chatham Island rubies' and 'emeralds' are crystals of red garnet and green pyroxene (enstatite) that are found on Pateriki Beach, in particular, as components in the sand. Superb large crystals of black or dark brown hornblende, found in Late Miocene and Pliocene volcanic rocks, particularly on Mangere and northwest Pitt Island, but also at Maunganui and Cape Young, are called 'Chatham Island diamonds'. Reports of gold, though plausible given the presence of schist with abundant quartz veins, remain unsubstantiated.

The most valuable rock types in the Chathams are those used in construction, roading and farming. They include schist, greywacke, volcanic rocks (mainly basalts), sand and limestone.

Tough rounded cobbles and pebbles of chert (flint) of many colours, textures and shapes are found on beaches and terraces in the Chathams, but particularly in northern Chatham Island. Artefacts, flakes and chips of the same tough, fine-grained siliceous rock types are also relatively common, and provide evidence that Moriori used them as cutting, scraping and flensing instruments before the arrival of the first Europeans and Maori.

These rocks are a geological curiosity because some of them are not known from any rock formation present on the Chathams today. They are interpreted as the remnants of limestones (probably of Oligocene to Miocene age, 34–5 million years old) that have been completely eroded. Some of these may also have been brought ashore by seals as gastroliths (rocks swallowed at sea as ballast and regurgitated on land). Some are clearly derived from the Taoroa Limestone of Early Miocene age (c.23 Ma) that is exposed only at the north end of Maunganui.

Other exotic rock types are found occasionally in the Chathams and have been introduced by humans as either cultural material (for example obsidian from North Island localities, and greenstone and argillite from the South Island) or ship ballast (slate from Wales). Pumice is relatively common on all coasts in the Chatham Islands, mostly derived from the Taupo Eruption 1800 years ago and continuing to wash up after having floated across from major river sources in the North Island. Some distinctive pumices are derived from elsewhere, such as the South Sandwich Islands far away in the south Atlantic Ocean.

Floating icebergs may also have transported foreign rock to the Chathams from Antarctica. Regular sightings of icebergs were reported

Opposite: A simplified geological map of the Chatham Islands showing the distribution of basement metamorphic rocks (Chatham Schist); the oldest 100–90 million-year-old sediments in the Chathams (Tupuangi Formation); the remnants of the Chatham Volcano, which erupted 85–80 million years ago (Southern Volcanics); the 'cover sediments' (limestones, greensands, tuffs, sands, peats) that have accumulated in the past 75 million years (Late Cretaceous to Cenozoic time); and the younger volcanic rocks (Northern Volcanics and Rangitihi Volcanics) of Eocene and Pliocene age respectively.

GNS Science

from the Chathams between 1850 and 1950. Mainland New Zealand rocks also reach Chatham shores in the root plates of trees washed out to sea during floods. A similar mechanism can redistribute local rocks, when bull kelp holdfasts are ripped off by storms and washed onto beaches.

Faults and earthquakes

No active faults are known in the Chathams, and indeed very few faults have been mapped. A major fault must be responsible for uplift of the basement Chatham Schist of northern Chatham Island, but it is not exposed. The structure of northern Pitt Island is more complex than Chatham, with numerous small faults and some folding that developed largely in response to the eruption of Mangere and associated volcanoes. A series of conspicuous normal faults can be seen in the coastal cliffs in Waihere Bay, displacing the well-exposed Tupuangi Formation succession of mid-Cretaceous age (100–90 Ma).

Earthquakes are felt occasionally in the Chathams, usually from large distant earthquakes such as the 6.8-magnitude earthquake that struck the Gisborne area on 20 December 2007. There is negligible seismic activity at the eastern end of the Chatham Rise, and no earthquake epicentres have ever been located within the Chatham Islands themselves. However, tsunamis generated by large earthquakes around the Pacific, especially adjacent to the coast of South America, pose a potential threat to low-lying areas of the Chathams. The only known tsunami-related death in New Zealand occurred at Tupuangi, northwest Chatham Island, in 1868, and was associated with a major earthquake off the coast of Chile.

Through much of Cenozoic time the islands did not exist: they became emergent only about 2.5 million years ago. The mechanism for uplift remains uncertain but most probably relates to a bulge within the Earth's mantle of regional extent. Furthermore, uplift may still be happening. Further geophysical investigations are required to resolve the mechanism.

The Chathams are more susceptible than most areas of New Zealand to the weather and the sea. However, the mantle of peat, that unique essence of the Chathams, has a calming effect, giving the appearance of a mature landscape and comparative stability.

Despite the tsunami hazard and susceptibility to erosion, the Chatham Islands may be regarded as the most stable part of New Zealand. The Chathams will persist, even with the potential threats of erosion, sea-level change and volcanic activity, and it is justifiable to think of the island group as a high point on the Chatham Rise that just happens to be above water at present.

The erosive effect of oceanic swells and prevailing southwesterly weather has produced cliffs around much of the Chatham Islands, such as these on Mangere Island.

Sönke Hardersen

CHAPTER THREE

MARINE LIFE

Everyone who lives on or visits the Chatham Islands feels a strong affinity to the sea. The ocean dominates the islands and their inhabitants. Like the tip of an iceberg, the islands sit above a vast undersea complex that is teeming with marine life. The marine environment extends from the wave-battered intertidal zone through coastal areas dominated by seaweed-covered rocky reefs and a few sandy lagoons, to the dark offshore abyss, with strange fishes and other creatures adapted to low light and cold, deep waters. From the earliest humans to current inhabitants, the history of the islands is essentially maritime, involving accommodation to the often harsh sea-dominated climate and weather conditions, and harvesting of vast quantities of marine animals for sustenance and economic livelihood.

The Chatham Islands are the emergent part of the Chatham Rise, which is a system of deep troughs descending to 2 kilometres below sea level, and steep sea mounts rising from the ocean floor. The islands sit along the Subtropical Front, a confluence of two water masses that greatly influences the diversity and character of marine life at the islands. Cool temperate water derived from the Southland Current, which flows around southern New Zealand, mixes with warmer subtropical water from the East Cape Current, providing conveyor-belts for northern and southern species to colonise the islands. Average surface sea temperatures around the islands vary seasonally from about 9 to 18°C. The sea around the islands is biologically productive because of upwelling of nutrient-

Top: **Kina (sea eggs) on the sea floor, Chatham Islands.** Malcolm Francis, NIWA

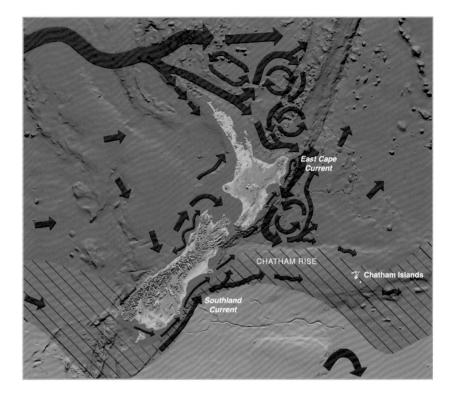

The Chatham Rise and the Chatham Islands straddle the Subtropical Front (hatched), an area where cold and warm currents meet.

NIWA

rich oceanic water, and is unusually clear because of the absence of coastal run-off from a large landmass.

The islands and islets together have around 400 kilometres of coastline. Chatham Island is by far the largest and best known. Its varied coastline provides different degrees of protection from wave exposure, and so harbours plants and animals adapted to conditions ranging from sheltered to extremely turbulent. The southern shore has cliffs several hundred metres high and is usually pounded by huge oceanic swells. The eastern side of the island is protected from southerly swells and has beaches and offshore sandy habitats, especially in Hanson Bay. The north coast is also semi-protected, has mixed rocky and sandy habitat, and is a prime area for the paua (*Haliotis iris*) fishery. The Port Hutt bays are protected inlets. The southwest coast around Cape L'Eveque to Point Durham is rocky and often has a refracted swell. Much of the west coast is taken up by Petre Bay, a long sweep of sandy shore. Just north of this bay is a series of basaltic pillars that extend subtidally at Ohira Bay.

Southern bull kelp (*Durvillaea antarctica*).

Graham Wood

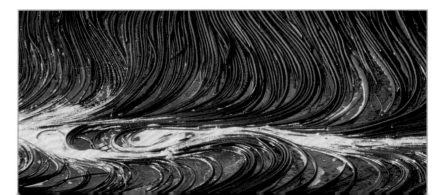

Pitt Island has rocky habitat around much of its coastline and, like Chatham Island, is very exposed to the south and more protected to the north. The Flower Pot area on the northwest coast is a favourite spot for fishing. Mangere Island has beautiful undersea habitat on its northern side. However, Pitt Strait can be extremely tumultuous as tide and swell often clash.

The habitats of the Chatham Islands are delineated by both their degree of exposure and the substratum types. Rocky habitats dominated by large beds of seaweeds occur on all coastlines of the Chathams. On extremely exposed southern shores, large brown algae occur only to about 10 metres depth. However, algal stands dominate from the low intertidal zone to more than 20 metres depth in more protected areas of the eastern, western and northern coastlines. Intertidal rocky platforms support dense aggregations of grazing invertebrates, filamentous, foliose and crustose algae, and dense beds of bull kelp (*Durvillaea* spp.) along the intertidal–subtidal margins.

Rocky shores

Algal beds and forests

At first glance the rocky shores of the Chatham Islands are similar to those of central and southern New Zealand. High to mid-intertidal areas are dominated by many small red and brown seaweeds, with invertebrates such as barnacles, limpets and chitons common. In exposed areas, particularly along the southern shores from Point Durham to Owenga and along the southern shore of Pitt Island and associated rocky outcrops, lower intertidal platforms are dominated by bull kelp. Fronds can reach 11 metres in length, and their whipping action in waves can scour an area bare on the rocks beneath them, leaving mainly limpets and encrusting red algae.

At around 2 to 5 metres depth, many boulders with a patchy cover of large brown seaweeds provide habitat for paua or abalone (*Haliotis* spp.), kina (sea eggs, *Evechinus chloroticus*) and other invertebrates. Down to 20 metres, lush seaweed beds form canopies a metre or so above the bottom. Many species of fish live in these algal beds. Deep reefs often have a dense cover of encrusting invertebrates. Rocky ground gives way to sand in most places at 20–25 metres. In more sheltered areas, such as the northwestern shore of Chatham Island at Waitangi West, western Cape Young, inside the Port Hutt bays and along northeastern Pitt Island, giant kelp forms dense forests with thick canopies floating on the sea surface. These create shade on the bottom, providing ideal conditions for understorey algae and encrusting invertebrates, particularly sponges. Divers in such forests experience the calm and twilight of terrestrial forests, but can move easily through all three dimensions.

Kina (*Evechinus chloroticus*).
Malcolm Francis, NIWA

Chatham Island bull kelp (*Durvillaea chathamensis*).
Malcolm Francis, NIWA

The endemic kelp *Lessonia tholiformis* forming a canopy over species of *Carpophyllum* and *Cystophora*, with an understorey of pink crustose coralline algae. Extreme low tide at Te Whakaru Island.

Peter de Lange

SEAWEEDS

Around 250 species of marine macroalgae have been found on the Chatham Islands, about 65 per cent of which are species of red algae. Seven species are considered endemic, but otherwise the seaweed flora contains both northern and southern New Zealand species, reflecting oceanographic influences. However, some common mainland species are absent, including the kelps *Ecklonia radiata* and *Lessonia variegata*, perhaps because they lack buoyancy for long-range dispersal.

In sheltered areas algal stands dominate from the low intertidal zone to more than 20 metres depth, with encrusting, filamentous and other understorey algae in addition to the more conspicuous brown algae that form the canopy structure. Large seaweeds form densely shaded beds along the shallow coastal reefs. Southern bull kelp (*Durvillaea antarctica*), which is distributed widely across southern New Zealand, the subantarctic islands and Chile, is common on the Chathams. A related endemic species, *D. chathamensis*, occurs lower on the shore and differs in having no buoyant honeycomb structure within its fronds to keep it afloat.

There are two true kelps found at the Chatham Islands. Giant kelp (*Macrocystis pyrifera*) occurs in thick beds along northeastern Pitt Island and in sheltered bays such as Port Hutt. The endemic leathery kelp *Lessonia tholiformis* is the only species of *Lessonia* present. It forms dense beds at depths of 2–15 metres, and is especially common around the Port Hutt bays and from Point Durham to Cape L'Eveque off southwest Chatham Island.

Many species of large brown seaweed, most without common names, are locally abundant. The endemic *Landsburgia myricifolia* reaches up to a metre in height and often forms dense beds, interspersed with the common oak-leaf alga of the New Zealand coast (*L. quercifolia*) at depths of 6–15 metres. *Xiphophora gladiata* is particularly common in the more sheltered areas around Ocean Bay, the Port Hutt bays and Point Gap, where it may cover 30 per cent of the bottom at a metre depth. Three of the four *Carpophyllum* species found on the mainland also occur at the Chathams. The flat-bladed *C. maschalocarpum* and the feathery *C. plumosum* reach over a metre in length and can cover more than 30 per cent of the bottom at 2–5 metres. They are particularly common in the most sheltered waters, where bull kelps are sparse, such as the Port Hutt bays and the north coast of Chatham Island. The most prominent is *C. flexuosum*, which can form extensive canopies 2 metres above the sea floor at depths of 6–15 metres in more sheltered waters, reaching densities of 45 plants per square metre. In exposed conditions, such as the coast near Point Durham, it is abundant only in deep water, presumably because it is susceptible to removal by waves.

Layered coralline red alga (*Mesophyllum erubescens*) growing in the upper subtidal zone under a canopy of brown algae (*Cystophora* and *Carpophyllum* species), Port Hutt.
Kate Neill

Calcified and crustose red algae are abundant in the Chatham Islands, and play an important role in the lives of many invertebrates. Dismissed in the past as 'pink paint', these crusts are now known to produce chemicals that promote settlement of larvae of some tubeworms, chitons, starfish, hard and soft corals, kina and paua.

The invasive Asian kelp *Undaria pinnatifida* has yet to establish on the Chathams, although juvenile plants were removed from the hull of *Seafresh 1*, which foundered off Owenga in 2000. This incident shows how vulnerable Chatham marine ecosystems are to foreign organisms arriving on fouled hulls and in ballast.

David Schiel & Wendy Nelson

Large paua are abundant in shallow subtidal waters, and are the basis of a lucrative fishery.

Reyn Naylor, NIWA

Grazing invertebrates

The most prominent grazers of the sea floor at the Chathams are paua, which still occur in large numbers. All three species of New Zealand paua (*Haliotis iris*, *H. australis*, *H. virginea*) occur at the Chathams, but by far the most abundant is the black-footed *H. iris*. Paua are most abundant in rocky habitats down to around 10 metres depth, but are found to 20 metres where reefs extend to deep water. The northern coast and the exposed south coast of Chatham Island have been very productive areas for the paua fishery. Before heavy fishing, paua were abundant in the low-intertidal zone and in tide pools, but this is no longer the case. Production of juveniles is prolific at the Chathams, and most inshore boulders will have several of them. Just turn over the rocks and watch the paua glide into cover. The shallow inner parts of the Port Hutt bays and just north of Owenga are good places to find juveniles. As paua mature (at around 70mm in length) they slowly migrate to deeper reefs, where they feed primarily on drift seaweeds.

Kina (common sea urchins) occur on most rocky shores around the islands. At the Chathams they do not seem to cause the 'underwater deserts' seen in northern New Zealand, the result of kina removing large algae and then grazing off any new plants that settle. Kina are fished commercially for their roe (gonads). Some scientists believe grazing by kina provides habitat on which paua can settle and grow. Others believe that the two compete for food because both are grazers. Kina are active grazers, able to remove large plants from the sea floor, while paua are passive grazers that trap drift algae brought to them by wave action. At the Chathams, kina are most abundant at 7–15 metres depth, where the abundance of paua declines. Kina are very abundant along the northern and exposed southern coast of Chatham Island.

Another prominent mobile invertebrate is Cook's turban shell (*Cookia sulcata*). This thick-shelled marine snail occurs from the low intertidal zone down to around 20 metres depth beneath seaweed canopies. It is very abundant around Kaingaroa, where vast numbers of shells are cast ashore.

Most of the marine invertebrates at the Chathams are shared with the mainland. There are more than 90 species of sea urchin, starfish, brittle star, feather star and sea cucumber. The majority of these range over the continental shelf from Cook Strait south. Crustaceans (including crabs and lobsters) also show a strong affinity with central and southern New Zealand. Because of the long larval life of many of these species, recruitment to the Chathams may come via currents flowing north along the Southland Front and east along the Chatham Rise. This contrasts with encrusting invertebrates such as sponges and ascidians (sea squirts), 40 per cent of which are endemic to the islands, probably because the adults and larvae cannot float and disperse far.

Reef fish

The fish fauna of the Chathams is diverse and shows the closest similarities to the fauna of the east coast of central New Zealand, with only 8 per cent northern and 4 per cent southern species. Around 300 of the more than 1000 species found around the mainland occur at the Chathams, and none is endemic. About 55 species occur in rockpool habitats, the most accessible areas for observing marine life. Triplefins ('cockabullies') are the most conspicuous of these.

To the diver and underwater naturalist the numbers and diversity of large mobile fishes are usually the main attraction of an underwater reef. Observers will not be disappointed anywhere at the Chathams where hard reefs and forests of large brown algae occur. These are nursery grounds for many fishes, which settle from the plankton into seaweed forests, feed on the small invertebrates on the seaweed fronds, and find shelter in the vertical structure afforded by these large algae.

Banded wrasse (*Notolabrus fucicola*).
Malcolm Francis, NIWA

Reef fishes tend to be associated with particular habitats and, as the structure of algal stands changes with depth, so the fish fauna changes as well. As on mainland coasts, wrasses are common in shallow water, where banded wrasses (*Notolabrus fucicola*), spotties (*N. celidotus*) and girdled wrasses (*N. cinctus*) glide above algal canopies. Concealed among algal fronds are juvenile butterfish (*Odax pullus*), which are long and thin and assume the colour of the algae, apart from a white stripe along the length of their bodies. Large numbers of butterfish occur at Mangere Island and in sheltered bays of Pitt Island, where surveys have recorded 21 individuals per 300 square metres in lush *Lessonia* stands. These fish feed mainly on the tender fronds and reproductive parts of inshore seaweeds. Large butterfish cruise within canopies, maintaining a home range for feeding on algae and breeding. Occasional marblefish (*Aplodactylus arctidens*) can be seen lazing on the sea floor, where they feed mostly on red seaweeds.

Juvenile butterfish (*Odax pullus*) among *Cystophora* sp.

Malcolm Francis, NIWA

At 5–10 metres depth algal beds become denser, and fish abundance and diversity increase. The wrasses increase in number, leatherjackets (*Parika scaber*) can be seen idling about the algal fronds, and larger bottom-feeding fishes such as blue moki (*Latridopsis ciliaris*) and tarakihi (*Nemadactylus macropterus*) meander just above the sea floor.

Of all the reef fishes, blue cod (*Parapercis colias*) are the most obvious and abundant at rocky sites, and even along sandy areas with sparse rock. They can reach average densities of 15 individuals per 300 square metres at 5–10 metres depth, and almost double this density in deeper water. However, these historically great abundances have been reduced by fishing pressure. Blue cod scuttle along the sea floor, only rarely rising above the bottom, where they prey on smaller fish such as triplefins, and invertebrates.

On deeper reefs (15-30 metres) blue cod, girdled wrasses and blue moki can be abundant. Butterfly perch (*Caesioperca lepidoptera*) drift in mid-water, while occasional hapuku (groper, *Polyprion oxygeneios*) majestically cruise by. Hapuku can reach over 1.5 metres in length and are common on deep offshore reefs.

On calm days the quiet inlets of the Port Hutt bays can be like large aquaria. Shafts of light play on the shallow underwater algal stands, while most of the common reef fishes swim in and out of view. These shallow reefs are among the relatively unknown treasures of New Zealand, with good underwater visibility and high diversity and abundance of reef organisms.

A cautionary note is warranted because the islands also have many horror stories involving sharks. Three attacks on paua divers created news sensations during 1993–96. Great white sharks (*Carcharodon carcharias*) and other sharks have circled and bumped divers and are commonly seen around the islands. It would be unwise to spearfish offshore in any area of the Chathams.

A great white shark attracted to the surface for tagging, off the Star Keys. Note the satellite tag already in place behind the dorsal fin.

Heather Fener

Soft shores

Despite the abundance of sandy shores at the Chathams, relatively little is known about their ecology. The most extensive soft shores are along Petre and Hanson Bays, and surf clams are abundant in many sandy areas. Tuatua (*Paphies subtriangulata*) are found at or below low tide on ocean beaches along the north coast of Chatham Island, and in Petre and Hanson Bays. There are reports of large populations of tuatua at Shelly Beach, near Owenga. In more sheltered areas of sand and mudflats, pipi (*Paphies australis*) can be seen at or below the mid-tide mark. Many other bivalves occur at the Chathams, but toheroa (*Paphies ventricosa*), the large and highly prized clams of the mainland, are notably absent.

Te Awapatiki, the outlet of Te Whanga Lagoon.

Peter Johnson

Te Whanga Lagoon

Te Whanga Lagoon, which occupies a sizeable portion of Chatham Island, is usually isolated from the sea, although its entrance is occasionally broken open by large storms or by bulldozing. The lagoon is probably most famous for the fossilised sharks' teeth that can be seen along the shoreline, particularly after sediments have been stirred by storms. In most places the lagoon itself is only a few metres deep, and the water is brackish. The most common fish are flounder, but larger species, including sharks, also enter at times. Horse's mane weeds (*Ruppia megacarpa* and *R. polycarpa*) grow prolifically in places, and are sought after by foraging black swans. The red alga *Gracilaria chilensis* is also abundant, along with filamentous species of *Callithamnion*, sea lettuce (*Ulva* spp.) and the introduced brown alga *Striaria attenuata*. Te Whanga is an important food source for local people, supplying notably eels, flounder (mainly sand flounder *Rhombosolea plebeia*), whitebait (common smelt *Retropinna retropinna* and juvenile *Galaxias* species), cockles (*Austrovenus stutchburyi*), and black swan eggs, but commercial harvest of any of these from the lagoon is forbidden.

The northern shore of Te Whanga Lagoon.

Dave Houston

Fisheries

Fisheries have been at the very core of the history of the Chathams. Moriori used seals, stranded whales and fish as sources of protein. Foreign sealers and whalers quickly followed the first European explorers in 1791. After the sealing and whaling era, settlers continued to come to the islands to take advantage of plentiful fish stocks, such as blue cod, working on fishing boats or in the associated fish-processing industry. By the late 1960s a crayfish (*Jasus edwardsii*) bonanza began, with a flotilla of boats descending on the islands, and within five years the resource was seriously depleted. More recently there has been sequential exploitation of fisheries for offshore species such as orange roughy, inshore fishes such as hapuku and blue cod, shellfish such as paua, scallops and kina, and ongoing but reduced harvest of crayfish. Some of these proved to be boom-and-bust fisheries: after a burst of vigorous activity some fisheries either collapsed or else persisted at much reduced levels. However, unlike the situation for Chatham Islands' birds, there are few known cases of sea animals being driven to extinction.

The Quota Management System now regulates all of the fisheries of the Chathams. Catch quotas are set for each species, and these are reviewed annually, based on the latest information on catch, fishing effort and the state of the stock. The 2008 Chatham Island Inshore Fisheries Plan aims to ensure the long-term sustainability and economic viability of fisheries resources. A sometimes heated issue remains, however, in that mainlanders hold much of the quota, and so a large portion of the profits from fisheries leaves the islands.

Marine mammals

The earliest commercial 'fishery' at the Chatham Islands was for New Zealand fur seals (*Arctocephalus forsteri*), which were hunted for their valuable hides. Sealing lasted from around 1804 to 1844, by which time local populations were depleted nearly to extinction. Attention then

Fur seals at Rangatira Island.

Helen Gummer

turned to whales, with southern right whales (*Eubalaena australis*) hunted from shore-based stations from around 1830 until their commercial depletion about 1841. Sperm whales (*Physeter macrocephalus*) were hunted from about 1840 until the mid-1880s. Catches diminished after the 1860s, and the extraction and refinement of petroleum products to replace whale oil, and development of plastics to replace baleen, saw an end to the era of initial exploitation of marine resources at the Chathams. Seal and whale populations are recovering, and it is now common to see these marine mammals around the coast.

Blue cod

The fortunes of blue cod (*Parapercis colias*) fishers have waxed and waned over much of the past 90 years. Blue cod have always been abundant around the Chathams, except in areas of over-fishing, but the economics of the fishery have often been marginal. Blue cod are readily caught, and they occur over virtually all rocky reef areas from shallow waters to around 50 metres depth. Like many other species at the Chathams they have been a boom-and-bust fishery, with high catches followed by depletion. The first major commercial fishery for blue cod began in 1932, when an enterprising group from England set up a company to target this species. They fished from Whangaroa (Port Hutt), working mainly around the western coastline and The Sisters. The Western Reef alone yielded over 1.5 million kilograms of cod before it was fished out. The cod bonanza lasted only a couple of years before easily fished reefs were depleted and the fleet had to go to more distant fishing grounds, such as Pitt Island, which entailed far more expense. After diminishing returns, the company finally went bankrupt in 1940.

The current Chatham annual quota for blue cod is 736 tonnes. Although cod are readily caught on hooks, the modern fishery uses

Owenga fishing fleet, 1933.

Sir Charles Fleming Collection,
Alexander Turnbull Library,
PA1-o-1319-39

Blue cod (*Parapercis colias*).
Malcolm Francis

mostly baited pots. The costs of fuel and running a boat to access fishing sites, and the variable selling price of the fish, have meant that even good catches of around a tonne per day are often only marginally profitable. Because of its abundance, ease of fishing and appealing taste blue cod is a mainstay of the local diet, but commercially it is mostly a filler species for those fishing other stocks.

Crayfish

Crayfish (or New Zealand rock lobster, *Jasus edwardsii*) had been caught in large numbers at the Chatham Islands by bottom trawlers as early as 1907. In 1923 a fisheries biologist stated that crayfish were 'not worth troubling about'. However, by the 1960s they certainly were, and a combination of high prices, a rapidly expanding coastal fishing fleet

The crayfish (rock lobster) fishery peaked in 1968, with 6000 tonnes reported caught.
Graham Wood

and the search for new fishable stocks led to the commercial rediscovery of 'crays' at the Chathams.

After 2 tonnes were landed in 1965 the fishery developed almost exponentially, reaching a peak of 5958 tonnes in 1968, with 120 vessels catching an average of 50 tonnes each. Up to 40 per cent of the catch was taken by trawling in the early period. The animals caught were large and represented an accumulated population of older individuals. The number of vessels continued to increase and the average landings declined rapidly. For example, 200 tonnes of crayfish were taken from one square kilometre near Green Point before it was fished out. By 1974 just 61 vessels were fishing, with an average annual catch of 8.5 tonnes, and most of the larger, older crayfish had disappeared. From a peak of almost 6000 tonnes in 1968, catches decreased to around 500 tonnes in 1974, and 360 tonnes in 2008.

Crayfish live on shallow rocky reefs, where they forage on invertebrates, such as snails and sea urchins, and also scavenge. They are readily attracted to baited pots, the chief method by which they are caught. They migrate seasonally between shallow and deep reefs (down to 100 metres) and occasionally move in large aggregations along the open sea floor. This enabled them to be captured easily in large numbers during the early period of the boom, when they were trawled in open areas of Hanson and Petre Bays. Crayfish have a nine-month larval life and become fishable at around seven years of age.

Crayfish are caught almost entirely in pots, although trawling produced large catches in the early days of the fishery.

Graham Wood

Orange roughy

Orange roughy (*Hoplostethus atlanticus*) are deep-water fish that occur in continental slope waters from around 800–1300 metres around much of New Zealand. The Chatham Rise is the most important fishery for this species in New Zealand, and one of the biggest in the world. Relatively small quantities were caught in the 1970s, but the fishery expanded rapidly to 10,500 tonnes in 1979, and reached 45,000 tonnes by 1983. The fishery requires sophisticated trawler technology to fish the great depths at which orange roughy live, and to withstand the severe sea conditions on the Chatham Rise. Like crayfish, orange roughy were heavily fished in their early years of exploitation. The fishery coincided with the declaration of the 200-mile Exclusive Economic Zone and a rise in price and demand for fillets. Orange roughy were caught in vast quantities because they form dense breeding aggregations. They are now known to grow slowly, become sexually mature at around 20 years, and live to more than 30 years. This makes orange roughy vulnerable to overfishing, and this has been recognised by lowering the quota. The current commercial catch quota around the Chathams is 10,500 tonnes annually.

Scallops

Perhaps New Zealand's shortest-lived fishery boom was the Chathams scallop (*Pecten novaezelandiae*) fishery. Areas in Hanson Bay and along the north coast were heavily fished for just three years (1988–1990), with annual catches of 121, 74 and 37 tonnes respectively. Although a quota of 23 tonnes was set for 2007, there was no commercial harvest that year.

Paua

Paua is the most accessible of all the valuable marine species. The biggest inshore fishery at the Chathams is for black-footed paua (*Haliotis iris*), which have become increasingly valuable for their shell and meat since the early 1980s. There are reports of several tonnes of paua being taken from a single tide pool on the Star Keys as recently as 1989. Dense aggregations of paua are still seen, but most are undersized, and many inshore patches have been depleted. Since 1990 there has been a 326-tonne commercial catch quota, but it is not yet clear whether this will be sustainable in the long term. Paua populations at the Chathams must be self-seeding because the larval life is so short (10–14 days) that larvae are unlikely to arrive from any mainland source.

A paua diver.
David Schiel

   Paua fishers at the Chathams were the first to attempt rejuvenating fished populations by reseeding them using hatchery-reared juveniles bred from native stock. The initial success of large-scale experiments around the Chathams in the late 1980s and 1990s led to reseeding operations being carried out in other parts of New Zealand. More recently the development of technology and methods for paua 'pearls', also known as 'mabe' or blister pearls, has added impetus to the paua industry. Implanted paua are grown in shore-based facilities or marine farms, usually in barrel culture, but there is only one experimental farm at the Chathams. The high value of paua meat (NZ$70–112 per kilogram), paua pearls (several hundred dollars each) and paua shell ensures that paua will remain a major fishery at the Chathams.

Kina

Kina, also known as sea urchins or sea eggs, are multi-spined echinoderms that can be abundant on rocky reefs. The common sea urchin of the Chathams and mainland New Zealand is *Evechinus chloroticus*, which often occurs in large aggregations (see page 53). They are mostly herbivorous, and eat almost any seaweed they encounter. Robust teeth on their bottom surface can chew through even the toughest of seaweeds, and they frequently scrape rocky reef surfaces to remove encrusting algae and invertebrates. Beyond their smaller juvenile stages, few predators are able to breach their spiny defences and eat them. One exception is the large sea-star (*Astrostole scabra*), which immobilises urchins and rolls them along its orange tube feet to be slowly consumed.

Kina occur all around the rocky reefs of the Chathams. They are prized for their roe, which consists of five fat strips lining the inside of their calcareous test (shell). Kina were part of traditional diets in the Chathams, but are an acquired taste! Sea urchins have been fished commercially worldwide since at least the 1950s, but more recently at the Chathams. The major fishery occurs along the more protected waters of the north coast. Kina are gathered off the sea floor using a hand-held hook, flicked into a bag and taken back to boat tenders. The roe yield of kina is up to 12 per cent of total body weight, and fishers are paid on roe recovery (in the order of NZ$7–8 per kilogram). The work is labour-intensive and the costs relatively high. As for some other inshore fisheries, kina are mainly a filler fishery for those fishing other stocks. The current annual commercial quota is 225 tonnes, less than half of which is actually fished.

Other commercial species

Many other species are economically important at the Chatham Islands. These include deep-water oreo dories (three species, with total quota in 2008 of 7000 tonnes), nearshore fishes such as blue moki (24 tonnes), sea perch (*Heliocolenus percoides*, 910 tonnes), tarakihi (316 tonnes), trumpeter (*Latris lineata*, 59 tonnes), butterfish (10 tonnes) and hapuku (322 tonnes), and invertebrates such as dredge oysters (*Ostrea chilensis*, 15 tonnes) and paddle crabs (*Ovalipes catharus*, 25 tonnes).

Recreational fishing and diving

The Chatham Islands provide a relatively wild wonderland for marine-based activities, yet have most of the conveniences of modern life. The diving is magnificent, particularly in the Port Hutt bays, where there is a good degree of protection from oceanic swells. Some of these areas

Hapuku (*Polyprion oxygeneios*).
Malcolm Francis

are accessible from nearby roads, so shore-based diving and fishing can be relatively easy. However, for those wishing to go further afield, local guidance will be necessary. A few locals run charter boats for fishing. These operate out of Owenga, Waitangi and Kaingaroa, and fish mainly for hapuku and blue cod. Dive-boat charters must be arranged in advance through local fishers or boat owners.

The key to visitors having successful marine experiences at the Chathams is to be adventure-minded and largely self-contained. Dive gear is generally not for hire on the islands, and filling of scuba bottles requires identifying and getting the assistance of local owners of compressors (furthermore, airlines will usually not transport filled scuba bottles). There are also concerns about the transport of noxious organisms to the islands. A paua virus from Australia has devastated some abalone fisheries overseas, and local paua divers have asked that wetsuits be thoroughly washed and dried in the sun to minimise the chances of the virus being brought to the islands.

What of the future?

Marine resources supporting fisheries, tourism, recreation and healthily functioning ecosystems are vital to the Chatham Islands. Around 11 per cent of the population is actively engaged in fishing, and much of the economy is sea-dependent. 'Sustainability' and 'planning' are the catchwords, signalling a strong awareness of what is at stake.

There is considerable debate about the consequences of overfishing and ways to prevent it. 'Non-commercial areas' have been established to provide some measure of protection for reef-dwelling species, and sites where locals and their guests can gather kai moana. Enhancement of paua populations has been trialled, and the quotas for commercial species are reviewed annually. While commercial fishing of wild stocks is expected to remain the mainstay of the marine economy, there is likely to be increasing emphasis on marine farming, adventure tourism and recreational pursuits.

CHAPTER FOUR

MARINE MAMMALS

Marine life around the Chatham Islands is invigorated by the Subtropical Front, as warm subtropical ocean currents from the north meet the colder and less saline subantarctic waters from the south. This is reflected in abundant sea life, including a large number of marine mammals, with 28 species recorded at the Chathams. The most numerous are fur seals, which are best seen at Point Munning, and pilot whales, which frequently strand on northern Hanson Bay, Petre Bay and other beaches.

New Zealand fur seal

New Zealand fur seals (*Arctocephalus forsteri*) are migratory and spend much of their life at sea, so the age groups and sex ratios found at the Chathams change seasonally. Adult females come ashore in mid-November and give birth mainly in December. The larger adult males, some of which exceed 2 metres in length, form harems from the breeding females, and chase off the subadult males and juveniles.

During the summer months bull fur seals lie ashore guarding their females vigilantly, with little if any feeding, and they lose a great deal of weight. Mating occurs only a week or so after the birth of the pups. The cows suckle their pups on shore and go to sea on feeding forays until the pups are old enough to go with them. Some pups remain in the rookeries for up to 10 months before moving away. The population reaches a peak in early January, then declines from late February, with numbers at their lowest in October, shortly before the breeding cycle resumes.

Top: **Bull elephant seal, Rangatira Island.** Helen Gummer

In 1981 Graeme Wilson estimated that there were about 2100 fur seals at the Chatham Islands, with about 40 at Point Munning, a few nearby at Te Whakaru and about 25 on Tupuangi-Moana Reef on the northwest coast. The main breeding colonies were on the offshore islands. Wilson estimated about 270 were present in several breeding rookeries on the Forty Fours, and 700 on The Sisters, but he was unable to access rookeries on Rangatira Island, The Pyramid, Star Keys and Eastern Reef. The overall seal population has increased considerably over recent decades, and they now breed again on Chatham Island, at Point Munning.

Fur seals were formerly much more numerous on the Chathams, visiting all rocky shores on the main island too. Their bones are common in some Moriori middens but almost entirely absent over wide areas, suggesting local rather than widespread importance in Moriori diet. Probably both fur seals and sea lions were valued more for their durable skins, which were worn as wind-breaking capes. William Baucke, who lived with Moriori from 1848, wrote a detailed account of the great care exercised by latter-day Moriori when sealing. Working silently at night, so as not to disturb the timid herds, they culled only one or two carefully selected seals. Scrupulous care was taken the next morning to remove the carcasses and to scrub clean all bloodstains so that the remaining seals would not abandon the site.

The foreign sealers who arrived at the Chatham Islands from about 1804 had no such concerns. Quickly and indiscriminately, they took as many fur seal skins (of adults, subadults and pups) as possible, in order to forestall any competitors who might follow them. The Chathams lay on the sealers' route to and from the enormously rich Antipodes and Bounty Islands sealing grounds. Foreign sealers soon swept clean the Chathams rookeries, probably before 1810. A brief revival of southern sealing occurred after 1820, with small gangs stationed – or marooned – on many of the smaller islands, including The Sisters and The Pyramid. But the number of skins taken was never very high, and the last recorded exports from the Chathams were small consignments in the mid-1840s.

By this time at least half a million fur seals had been killed at the New Zealand subantarctic islands, and the population structure was so disrupted that it has taken 150 years for them to recover even half their former numbers. It is ironic therefore that the fur seal is the most conspicuous Chathams marine mammal today. Dozens can be seen in most seasons at Point Munning, with hundreds there in midsummer. This is private land, so permission must be obtained first.

Once at the rookery, visitors must respect the seals too. Noise and sudden movement will cause these timid animals to scamper off. It must be emphasised that all seal species are fully protected.

Fur seal pup, Rangatira Island.
Graham Wood

Fur seal tangled in trawl netting. All seals are fully protected by law, but this does not prevent some being killed or injured by modern fishing methods.
Graham Wood

New Zealand sea lion, female and male.

Colin Emslie

Other seal species

Although their bones are relatively common in some Moriori middens, New Zealand sea lions (*Phocarctos hookeri*) are seldom seen on Chathams coasts today. A young sea lion was on Rangatira Island in January 2002, and there are unconfirmed reports from near Owenga. The adult male sea lion is heavily built, with long dark brown hair, especially about the neck and shoulders. It is this distinctive mane that prompted the name 'sea lion', and also the alternative name 'hair seal'. The female is smaller, sleeker and cream or grey in colour.

Sea lions are very mobile on land, moving about on all four flippers, much like the related fur seal. They differ in this respect from the leopard seal (*Hydrurga leptonyx*), which also visits the Chatham Islands irregularly, hauling out on sandy beaches. Leopard seals can grow up to 2.5 metres long and have elongated bodies that they cannot lift off the

Leopard seal, Waitangi, September 2002.

DOC

ground except by arching their backs. They have a nasty bite and can move quickly; all seal species are best given a wide berth.

Another occasional visitor is the southern elephant seal (*Mirounga leonina*), a huge, clumsy, cigar-shaped animal that can grow to over 5 metres long. Its tough wrinkled hide is elephant-like, but the common name is usually attributed to the nose of the adult male, which, when the animal is disturbed or angry, can be distended like a small trunk. Elephant seals were killed by Moriori for their thick blubber, but were probably never numerous on the Chatham Islands. Nowadays, singles or pairs are seen occasionally. A mother and her pup were on the western shore of Te Whanga Lagoon in June 1965, and another pup was born south of Red Bluff in October 2006.

Bull elephant seal, Rangatira Island, October 1989.
Ron Nilsson, DOC

Female elephant seal and pup, south of Red Bluff, October 2006.
Dave Houston

Subadult male subantarctic fur seal, an occasional visitor to the Chathams. Rangatira Island, April 2003.

Elwyn Wilson

The fifth seal species that occasionally reaches the Chatham Islands is the distinctively marked subantarctic fur seal (*Arctocephalus tropicalis*), which is mainly found in the South Atlantic and southern Indian Oceans. These 'pale-faced' seals associate with their New Zealand fur seal cousins, and up to three at a time have been seen among the fur seals on Rangatira Island since 1996, and at Point Munning in 2008.

Sperm whale

For 50 years, from 1835 to 1885, the Chatham Islands attracted whaling ships from around the globe. Most vessels cruised between the Chathams and New Zealand, with the sperm whale (*Physeter macrocephalus*) their main prey. A particular feature of the Chathams grounds was the high proportion of large blubber-rich solitary males encountered there.

Sperm whales normally frequent deep waters, diving hundreds or even thousands of metres for squid. Thomas Ritchie, an early settler who lived on Chatham Island from 1864, described the best whaling grounds as lying 'on a line south-east of Pitt Island'. A whaler should 'commence within sight of Pitt Island, then south-east till the Pyramid almost drops out of sight, then about ship and cruise back to the starting point. There and nowhere else did [the last whalers] lay back and forward till the whales came.'

Historical records reveal over 250 visits by whaling ships. Logbooks and journals survive for about 120 of their cruises, and suggest that the total catch of sperm whales by sail-powered ships at the Chathams was probably close to a thousand. This 'harvesting' made sperm whales scarce, and their numbers declined very sharply in the early 1900s when steam-powered fleets swept subantarctic waters so thoroughly that few animals survived. Today only occasional sperm whales are sighted at

Sperm whale, north of Point Durham, December 2007. This animal spent a week close to shore in shallow water before heading back to sea.

Dale Williams

the Chathams. The blunt rectangular head and asymmetrical blowhole of this impressive animal are unmistakable, as is its distinctive high forward-angled spout.

Right whale

The other species sought by the sail whalers after 1830 was the southern right whale (*Eubalaena australis*). Almost a quarter of its body length consists of its huge rounded head, split by a great curving mouth. This is full of plates of coarse, hair-like baleen through which it strains water to obtain the tiny krill that are its main food. Right whales have a distinctive V-shaped double spout.

In earlier times, right whales often came close inshore, possibly to scrape barnacles from their backs. They followed regular migratory routes each winter, and by 1840 whalers had set up four stations on the Chatham Islands to kill right whales from the shore. So rapacious were these shore whalers and the ships cruising offshore that within six short winter seasons, from 1835 to 1841, right whales were almost exterminated from the seas around New Zealand.

The pitifully small remnant that survived into the 20th century was further reduced by steam-powered whalers and, only a few decades ago, fears were held for the survival of this species. Fortunately, breeding groups survived off the subantarctic Campbell and Auckland Islands, and nowadays a few right whales are reported along the New Zealand coast each winter. One photographed off Owenga in January 2003 was the first modern record from the Chatham Islands.

Southern right whale, Owenga, January 2003.

Anne Gregory-Hunt

Whale strandings

The Chatham Islands have a high frequency of whale strandings, with 22 species recorded. By far the most common species to strand is the long-finned pilot whale (*Globicephala melas*), known locally as blackfish, which is cast ashore in large numbers every year or so. Mass strandings on sandy beaches between Waitangi and Te One, and particularly in the remarkable 'whale graveyard' at the south end of Waikeri Beach (northern Hanson Bay), have prompted various theories. These include that gently shelving beaches disrupt their echo-location system, or that mass strandings occur when other whales try to assist ill or injured members of their pod. But why mass strandings occur so often at the Chatham Islands remains unclear.

The world's largest stranding of whales occurred on Long Beach in 1918, when about a thousand long-finned pilot whales came ashore. In former years attempts were made to cut up stranded blackfish and rend down the blubber into oil, but this entailed a huge mess and little profit for a very unpleasant task. Stranded pilot whales are now generally given a wide berth until the carcasses have rotted away.

Sperm whales frequently strand on the Chatham Islands, including 20 animals at Ngatikitiki in March 2000. Their enormous size is apparent from the huge skulls and vertebrae still lying on the beach.

At least eight species of beaked whale have stranded on the Chatham Islands, some of which are very rare and poorly known. Two species have been described from specimens from the Chatham Islands: Gray's beaked whale (*Mesoplodon grayi*) and the spade-toothed whale (*Mesoplodon traversii*). Although Gray's is the most frequently recorded beaked whale in the Chathams and New Zealand generally, beaked whale strandings are relatively rare.

All whale strandings, whether of living or dead animals, should be reported immediately to the Department of Conservation.

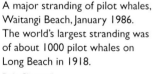

A major stranding of pilot whales, Waitangi Beach, January 1986. The world's largest stranding was of about 1000 pilot whales on Long Beach in 1918.

Rob Chappell

CHAPTER FIVE

MAJOR LAND HABITATS

The Chatham Islands are a world distinct from mainland New Zealand. Many of the islands' native plants and animals are found nowhere else, and many mainland plants and animals are absent. The land that the plants and animals inhabit is just as distinct. Long curving coastlines of white sand, massive volcanic cliffs, the huge Te Whanga Lagoon, lakes of all sizes and expansive undulating stretches of peat meeting dune sands from the shore: all contribute to a unique landscape.

Like mainland New Zealand, these islands were once part of the ancient continent of Gondwanaland. However, while the basement rocks may be up to 160 million years old, the islands are now believed to have been submerged until only 2.5 million years ago, with no land connection to mainland New Zealand. This may explain why so many plants and animals whose ancestors may have been on the original landmass are now missing from the Chathams region: kiwi and moa, wrens and wattlebirds, *Aptornis* rails and kakapo, large land snails, frogs, tuatara and geckos, southern conifers and beeches, and other trees such as tawa, pukatea, hinau, kamahi and rata. Many of these plants and animals have a very limited capacity to cross large stretches of water, so that, if they were ever present, there would be little chance of their reaching the Chatham Islands again.

Whatever the reason for their absence, these gaps in the flora and fauna mean that the plants and animals that did establish on the Chathams developed without some of the competitors present on the

Top: **Waipaua coast, Pitt Island.** Peter Johnson

Low vegetation, including a
flowering shrub of keketerehe
(*Olearia chathamica*), on the
'clears' of Rangatira Island.

Graham Wood

mainland. Thus most of the major trees and shrubs, as well as many
smaller plants, birds and invertebrates, have evolved as species that are
distinct from their mainland ancestors. They are endemic; that is, they
are found nowhere else. The resulting plant and animal communities are
also unique to these islands.

Another of the islands' distinguishing features is that they lie across
the Subtropical Front, a shifting boundary separating cold subantarctic
water from warmer subtropical water. The cold water is more nutrient-
rich and therefore supports greater numbers of marine organisms, some
of which become food for seabirds. Prior to human occupation, the
seabird population of the island group was enormous, as is demonstrated
by the distribution and abundance of subfossil bones in the older dunes.
Studies have suggested that the archipelago was once one of the most
important breeding stations in the world for petrels.

The forces that shaped the original pattern of plant and animal life
on these islands are varied and still at work. The land is largely low-lying,
without large climatic differences from place to place. Temperatures are

Chatham Island akeake (*Olearia traversii*) shaped by prevailing southwest winds, Point Weeding.
Dale Williams

cool, with a year-round average of about 11°C, ranging from 7.5° in July to 14° in January. Frosts are infrequent and generally light. Annual rainfall at Waitangi varies from 500 to 1000 millimetres, with more on the southern tableland. Dry spells are common, sometimes lasting more than a month. Skies are often overcast, with clear days averaging fewer than 70 a year. Humidity is high, commonly exceeding 80 per cent.

The prevailing southwest winds, frequently of gale force, are perhaps the most striking feature of the climate. These winds are often dry enough to pick up vast quantities of salt particles from breaking waves, perhaps far out at sea, and hurl them with great velocity at any exposed foliage. Few if any other places in the New Zealand region are so strongly influenced by wind-driven salt.

Last stage of a dying akeake, kopi (*Corynocarpus laevigatus*) and matipo (*Myrsine chathamica*) forest near Taupeka, Chatham Island. Wind and salt have killed most of the upper foliage, and grazing by stock prevents replacement by young trees.
Ian Atkinson

Part of northern and central Chatham Island has been flooded by the sea. Barriers of sand have then built up between areas of harder rocks to entrap the enormous Te Whanga Lagoon (18,300 hectares). Sand eroded from the coastal rocks, and derived also from seashell fragments, is piled into moving dunes that may sometimes elongate inland to bury mineral or peaty soils beneath.

Peat has been forming in the Chatham Islands for thousands of years, presumably because of the cool moist climate and gentle slopes. It appears to develop beneath both tarahinau forest and *Sporadanthus* rushlands. The oldest peats, particularly in the northwestern part of Chatham Island, have developed to the consistency of boot polish, with the properties of a young lignite. Peat may accumulate in hollows or, through continuous addition of decaying stems and leaves, form into large, gently sloping domes. These sometimes become unstable to the point where slumping reshapes their surface, leading to the formation of small lakes or tarns. Lightning-induced fires affected the Chathams landscape long before the arrival of humans, and subterranean peat fires can burn for years. Collapse of peat following such fires may have formed some of the lakes in the peat country.

With the arrival of Moriori, fires became more frequent, and still more so following European contact. Introduced animals and plants, particularly pigs, sheep, cattle, possums, cats, rats, mice, gorse and Chilean guava, as well as farming and roading have together greatly altered the original pre-human pattern of plant/animal communities. The dune forests were once dominated by Chatham Island akeake (*Olearia traversii*) and matipo (*Myrsine chathamica*), and together with Chatham Island karamu (*Coprosma chathamica*), lancewood or hoho (*Pseudopanax chathamicus*), and ribbonwood (*Plagianthus regius* subsp. *chathamicus*), these species were also the mainstay of forests on the volcanic soils.

Such forests once teemed with invertebrate life, including beetles and weta. Although several now-extinct ground birds, including the giant Hawkins' rail, would have fed on larger insects, the Chathams communities had no predatory reptiles such as tuatara, geckos or large skinks. The vestige of this amazing forest-floor community survives now only on Rangatira Island.

Where peat was forming, rushlands or shrublands of *Sporadanthus* and inaka (*Dracophyllum scoparium*) are likely to have been dominant. Where the peat dried out, and also on low-fertility mineral soils, tarahinau (*Dracophyllum arboreum*) was the major forest tree. Thus the vegetation of the southern tableland formed a mosaic of rushland, shrubland and forest, related to peat doming and fires. The immense colonies of burrowing seabirds were concentrated in a zone of high soil fertility that included older dunes and mineral soils in the northern half of Chatham Island and continued as a perimeter zone around the southern tableland behind the sea cliffs.

Although the earlier pattern of plant and animal distribution is now disrupted, its imprint is still expressed in the remaining native vegetation and in the residual fertility of the soils that were once so densely burrowed by seabirds. The perimeter zone contains some of the most fertile land for farming in these islands.

Coastal cliffs and rocky shorelines

Sweeping stretches of white sandy beach interspersed with cliffs or rocky shorelines characterise the northern coastline of the main island. In the south, beyond Waitangi and Owenga, are spectacular cliffs and a giant slump called Te Awatapu. Castle-like cliffs are also prominent along the southern part of Pitt Island and parts of Mangere and Rangatira Islands, and completely surround Little Mangere Island.

These coastlines, often with rocky shore platforms, include a mixture of stable and unstable sites. The massive rocks that form the cliffs and bluffs are relatively stable, even though they can be undermined by the constant pounding of waves. The intervening steep slopes of unconsolidated rock debris are often quite unstable.

Various plants of the coastal zone are able to establish on these different substrates, some being more suited to one kind of site than others. Close to the shoreline the salt from wave splash prevents many plants from growing. In this zone, however, are carpets of salt-resistant Chatham Island iceplant (*Disphyma papillatum*), both pink- and white-flowered forms, and glasswort (*Sarcocornia quinqueflora*). Here, too, are woody plants able to tolerate occasional wetting with salt water, such as endemic species of harakeke (flax; *Phormium* aff. *tenax*), hokataka (*Corokia macrocarpa*) and Chatham Island akeake, plus matipo.

Flowering Chatham Island iceplant (*Disphyma papillatum*), Mangere Island.
Rod Morris, DOC

Beyond the splash zone these plants remain abundant, except for glasswort, but are joined by several endemic species: the grasses *Poa chathamica* and *Festuca coxii*, the Chatham Island geranium (*Geranium traversii*), coxella (*Aciphylla dieffenbachii*), Chatham Island koromiko (*Hebe chathamica*) and keketerehe (*Olearia chathamica*). The endemic kakaha (*Astelia chathamica*) can still be found in places inaccessible to cattle, pigs and sheep, particularly along the south coast of Chatham Island. Many plants of the mainland New Zealand coast are missing from this coastal zone: taupata (*Coprosma repens*), species of five-finger and pittosporum, and small-leaved pohuehue (*Muehlenbeckia complexa*). Introduced taupata and karo (*Pittosporum crassifolium*) are now spreading out from most human settlements and invading native Chatham Island coastal plant communities.

Distant from the main islands are the small outliers: The Sisters, Forty Fours, Star Keys and The Pyramid. All are inhabited by seabirds, three of them supporting large colonies of surface-nesting albatrosses and giant petrels. The plant cover is modified by both extremes of wind and wind-driven salt, and by the fertilising and trampling of these very large seabirds. Plants are usually sparse, but a large groundsel (*Senecio radiolatus*) grows in loose soil, and the now-rare Chatham Island button-daisy (*Leptinella featherstonii*) is dominant, rooted in rocky crevices.

Dunelands

Dunes are one of the most dynamic land habitats, and a coastline such as that of Long Beach provides opportunity to see their ever-changing communities. Sand produced by the constant pounding of waves on rocks is carried to beaches from where it is blown landwards to form mounds and ridges that change continually in shape and position. Pingao (*Desmoschoenus spiralis*), originally the major sand-binding sedge (there

Chatham Island button-daisy (*Leptinella featherstonii*) is typically found at sites with large seabird populations providing abundant phosphates and nitrates. Rangatira Island.

Colin Miskelly

Pingao (*Desmoschoenus spiralis*) and Chatham Island sow thistle (*Embergeria grandifolia*) on foredunes, Kaingaroa.

Peter Johnson

A seedling of sand coprosma
(*Coprosma acerosa*) establishing
on 'raw' sand at Henga, Chatham
Island.

Ian Atkinson

is no spinifex grass in the Chathams), has been largely replaced by introduced marram grass (*Ammophila arenaria*).

As the sand begins to consolidate, knobby clubrush (*Ficinia nodosa*) and shrubs such as toroheke (sand daphne; *Pimelea arenaria*) and sand coprosma (*Coprosma acerosa*) establish. The endemic geranium and *Lobelia arenaria* appear in damp hollows. With further consolidation, dune mingimingi (*Leucopogon parviflorus*) and hokataka enter and often become dominant in shrubland. All these plants may be buried or excavated as sand is either deposited or blown inland.

Further from the Long Beach shoreline, sand has a greater chance of being stabilised. Beginning on the beach one can walk inland through marram grassland, then a mosaic of shrublands and eroding sand, and on into scrub and forest. The first trees to establish in the shrublands are akeake and mahoe (*Melicytus chathamicus*), then karamu, matipo and

Profile of the coastal dune
community at Long Beach,
Chatham Island. I: marram grass
on foredune; 2: dune hollow
with blow-out; 3: dune shrubland
and scrub of toroheke and dune
mingimingi; 4: stunted scrub and
forest of akeake and matipo
streamlined by wind-driven salt;
5: dune forest (A = akeake,
H = hoho, K = kopi,
Km = karamu, M = mahoe,
Mp = matipo).

Ian Atkinson

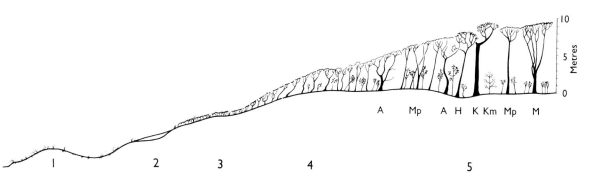

kopi (*Corynocarpus laevigatus*). The grey and twisted trunks of akeake characterise the dune forests, although in many places, as a result of browsing by stock, all that remain are scatterings of old trees.

The effects of wind-driven salt show in the tight and often furrowed canopy of the dune forests throughout the Chathams. These are stunted near the shore but increase steadily in height further inland. Most species have features that minimise salt damage to young buds. The buds of Chatham Island akeake, hokataka and keketerehe are surrounded by erect leaves, felted underneath with fine whitish hairs that form a salt barrier. The leaves of karamu are rolled so that the bud is protected, and the leaves of both matipo and kopi have heavy waxy surfaces that impede salt entry.

Dunes are an important breeding habitat for the endangered Chatham Island oystercatcher, formerly widespread around the coast. Grazing by stock has largely eliminated the original, more open dune community of pingao and endemic herbs such as Chatham Island forget-me-not (*Myosotidium hortensia*) and sow thistle (*Embergeria grandifolia*), and has allowed marram grass to form a closed cover. This kind of cover is not favoured by oystercatchers for nesting and has sometimes forced the birds to nest on the beach itself, where their eggs and young are vulnerable to storm waves or predation by cats or weka.

Volcanic hills and lowlands

Most of the once-forested volcanic hills and intervening shrublands and rushlands of northern Chatham Island are now pasture, bracken fernland and gorse scrub. In low-fertility areas bracken (*Pteridium esculentum*) forms a patchwork with tangle fern (*Gleichenia dicarpa*) and *Baumea* sedges. Where not recently burnt, inaka overtops the tangle fern, forming shrublands. These places include many peaty areas, the 'clears', although originally they were dominated by *Sporadanthus* bamboo-rush.

In spite of the long history of fires and firewood-cutting, forest remnants are scattered throughout the Chathams. On Chatham Island these remnants are characterised by kopi, matipo, karamu and akeake, with the latter two species being particularly common in swampy places. Hoho is widely distributed; nikau (*Rhopalostylis sapida*), Chatham Island ribbonwood and kowhai (*Sophora chathamica*) are more localised. Ribbonwood is abundant only in places of high fertility, particularly where burrowing petrels are or were present, or on limestone. Kowhai is mostly confined to old Maori settlement sites on limestone along the western side of Te Whanga Lagoon.

Chatham Islands matipo, karamu, akeake and kopi – some up to 20 metres tall – are also the major trees in forest remnants on Pitt Island. However, on the more peaty soils of southern Pitt, inland from Glory

Bracken fern (*Pteridium esculentum*) and the brighter green tangle fern (*Gleichenia dicarpa*) cover extensive areas of low-fertility soils on northern Chatham Island.

Colin Miskelly

Bay, tarahinau is the dominant forest tree. Abundant young trees of this and other species are establishing within areas that have been fenced and cleared of stock.

Although kopi (the karaka of mainland New Zealand) is prominent now in the Chatham lowlands, this may not always have been so. Moriori claim to have brought it to the Chathams, and the name kopi was used for the kernels of karaka fruit by at least one tribe in the southern North Island. Remains of kopi, such as pollen and seeds, have not been recovered from peats at any depths below the surface layer. And, unlike the majority of Chatham trees, it has not developed characteristics that distinguish it from the mainland karaka. All this implies it is a comparatively recent arrival.

After nikau, kopi is the tallest native tree in these islands, and perhaps this fact, together with its bark characteristics, influenced Moriori to use the trunks for carving their rakau momori. But how is it that these carvings have persisted for 200 years or more, when growth expansion of the trunk should have broken them up?

In many parts of the island where tree growth is relatively rapid, rakau momori apparently have disappeared (although they would not have been present originally at all sites), and other carvings can be found in a very poor state of preservation. At Hapupu, soils are shallow and dry out badly at times, with the result that tree growth is slow. This is perhaps the reason rakau momori are better preserved here than elsewhere.

Most forest remnants in the Chathams have been deteriorating steadily for the past 170 years. Fires, and sometimes felling for fenceposts and firewood have destroyed the streamlined forest margins,

Fence at Thomas Mohi Tuuta (Rangaika) Scenic Reserve, showing regeneration after exclusion of farm stock.

Colin Miskelly

Forest with dense fern undergrowth on the Tuku-a-tamatea River, Chatham Island. This is how most of the islands' deeper valleys would have appeared before they were cleared.

Colin Miskelly

leaving the windward side of the forest canopy exposed to dry salty winds that, gale by gale, eat their way through the forest. If stock are grazing beneath, there is no chance of replacement of the old trees when they die. However, enough places have now been fenced from stock to demonstrate the enormous capacity of Chatham forest plants to recover when given the chance.

Cattle, sheep and pigs are not the only introduced animals to destroy young trees. Possums, widespread on Chatham Island, eat seedlings as well as foliage, buds, flowers, fruit and bark. They can have marked effects on trees such as hokataka and rautini (*Brachyglottis huntii*), and the fruit crops of hoho. This fruit is a major food for parea when rearing young, and recent studies indicate that their breeding success is greatly reduced in some years as a result of browsing of hoho by possums.

In addition to the larger mammals, several predatory mammals have been purposely or accidentally introduced to the Chatham Islands. Cats, kiore, Norway rats, ship rats and mice all prey on birds, lizards and insects. Possums also eat birds' eggs and chicks, and pigs are serious predators of burrowing seabirds. The impact of hedgehogs on Chatham Island invertebrates and ground-nesting birds has not been studied. Weka, part of the endemic heritage of mainland New Zealand, were introduced to the Chathams in 1905, creating a new threat to the islands' birds and other animals. The native animals surviving on Chatham and Pitt Islands are those that have survived the impact of these introduced predators.

The zone of mineral soils around the fringes of Chatham Island and over much of Pitt Island includes some of the best farming land in the region. This is the zone once inhabited by millions of burrowing seabirds. It seems likely that these have left a ghostly imprint through the residual effects of the huge quantities of nutrients they brought to the islands from the sea.

Peaty uplands

The peaty uplands forming the southern part of Chatham Island, south from the Tuku-a-tamatea River to The Horns and Green Point, are not easily accessible. These southwestern uplands are hilly and covered by tarahinau forest up to 15 metres high. A thick carpet of tarahinau leaves covers the ground, often obscuring the surface, which has been ploughed by pigs searching for roots and invertebrates.

This is the only known breeding place for the few surviving taiko (Magenta petrels). Before fencing was completed, sheep, cattle and pigs wandered through this forest, so depleting it of young trees that replacement of mature trees was dependent largely on seedlings that established as epiphytes on tree-fern trunks (mainly *Dicksonia* spp.). Tree ferns themselves are relatively unpalatable, with the result that the

Left: Tarahinau (*Dracophyllum arboreum*) forest covers much of southern Chatham Island, including the Tuku Nature Reserve.

Colin Miskelly

Right: Young hoho (*Pseudopanax chathamicus*) establishing as an epiphyte on a wheki-ponga (*Dicksonia fibrosa*). Establishment on tree ferns is a common method by which trees palatable to farm and feral stock can escape browsing and grow to maturity.

Peter Johnson

forest in some valleys is dominated by their thick fibrous trunks and symmetrical crowns.

The more extensive eastern uplands extend from the tableland surrounding Lakes Rakeinui and Te Rangatapu to the catchment of Mangahou Creek. This land is covered by a mosaic of fernland (bracken with inaka and tangle fern), rushlands dominated by *Sporadanthus*, inaka and Chatham Island aster (*Olearia semidentata*), and patches of tarahinau forest. This vegetation is largely fire-induced, the deep-rooted *Sporadanthus* being able to recover more rapidly than woody species after burning. In the absence of further fires, the inaka overtops the *Sporadanthus* and tarahinau begins to establish.

Bracken and pouteretere (*Leptecophylla robusta*) characterise the shallow peats that once supported mixtures of tarahinau and broader-leaved trees. On deeper peats with water tables far below the surface, bracken and tangle fern have replaced the former tarahinau forest. On the very deep peats that form the peat domes, where the water table

Profile of vegetation on the southern tablelands, Chatham Island. 1: tall *Sporadanthus* rushland with Chatham Island aster and inaka growing on a dome of deep peat; 2: recently burnt peat slope with regenerating *Sporadanthus* at right, and a fernland of bracken, tangle fern and inaka at left; 3: inaka scrub developed after an earlier fire; 4: tarahinau forest on shallow peat over mineral soil. The tree ferns are wheki-ponga (thick trunks) and wheki (*Dicksonia squarrosa*; slender).

Ian Atkinson

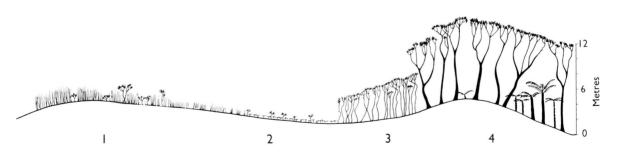

is near the surface, the *Sporadanthus*/inaka communities described above are dominant. If the water table is very close to or at the surface, sphagnum moss is likely to be vigorous, sometimes invading nearby tarahinau forest and killing trees along its margin.

Restoring lost habitats

We can never cease to regret that so much of the original wildlife and plant cover of the Chatham Islands has been lost or severely depleted. But this should not blind us to the possibilities of restoring some kinds of damaged habitat.

Islands such as Rangatira and Mangere must be kept free from too much human disturbance and from alien pests such as rats, mice, cats, wasps, gypsy moths and introduced weeds. Such islands are reservoirs of Chatham plants and animals from which something of the past can be rebuilt.

This process has already begun with restoration of forest on Mangere Island. It could continue with eradication or control of cats, pigs and weka on Pitt or on parts of Chatham Island. This would make possible the re-establishment of some of the rarer endemic plants, birds and other animals on the larger islands. Colonies of muttonbird (titi) could be established on headlands fenced to exclude predators. Judging by the growing albatross colony at Taiaroa Head, on the Otago Peninsula, the re-establishment of toroa (royal albatross) on Pitt Island, where they once bred, may be feasible.

Unlike the lifeless relics of a museum, living organisms in one place can be recombined to build functioning communities of plants and animals in another place.

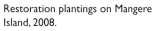

Restoration plantings on Mangere Island, 2008.

Bridget Gibb

CHAPTER SIX

FRESHWATER WETLANDS

Wetlands are both numerous and extensive on the Chatham Islands. The low-lying topography creates conditions of poor drainage, favouring wetland development not only in hollows and basins but also across tracts of tableland and gently rolling landscape. As a result of wet soil conditions, combined with the mild, moist oceanic climate, peat has accumulated across much of the land: almost 60 per cent of Chatham Island, and about 30 per cent of Pitt Island. The oldest peat on the Chathams – that at the base of the profile – is over 350,000 years old, and the peat sequence, along with its preserved plant spores and pollen, has much to tell us about history of climate, vegetation and fire. This story is supported by the layers of tephra of known age that originated as air-fall deposits from volcanic eruptions in the North Island.

Peat is made of dead plant material that has not completely decomposed. In soils that are often saturated, the discarded leaves and the dead twigs, roots and rhizomes of plants are not fully broken down by the action of fungi and bacteria, so all this material keeps accumulating beneath the vegetation. Peat on the Chathams reaches depths of up to 6 metres.

Although most Chatham wetlands have peat soils, many also have partly mineral soils containing silt or sand. The resulting variation in soil fertility – or nutrient status – leads to many distinct types of wetland. At one end of the spectrum, very infertile bogs sit upon pure peat in upland sites and across hill crests and broad basins. Bogs, by definition, are fed

Bog system at Waihi, within a large low-lying basin. Most of the bog is dominated by a brownish swathe of Chatham Island bamboo-rush (*Sporadanthus traversii*), while the drier portions hold sedgeland of the paler knobby clubrush (*Ficinia nodosa*).

Peter Johnson

Top: Black swans on Lake Marakapia. Peter Johnson

only by rainwater and not by groundwater that has been in contact with nutrient sources from underlying rocks. By contrast, in valley floors there are swamps where the peats have a component of silty material, along with inputs of groundwater and hillside runoff, and are therefore much more fertile. Between these extremes there are other wetland types, especially fens (peatlands on slight slopes), seepages (with peat or mineral soils on steeper slopes or in gullies), and marshes (on mainly mineral soils of gentle slope). In addition numerous dune lakes, peat lakes, ponds and streams each have their own type of wetland and aquatic vegetation. Then there is the massive Te Whanga Lagoon, some 20 per cent of the area of Chatham Island, which, although mainly saline or in parts brackish, is fringed with zones of freshwater wetland.

Chatham Islands wetlands are dominated by plants found nowhere else in the world. The importance of wetlands on the Chathams is illustrated by the fact that of the 392 native vascular plants, some 52 per cent extend into wetland habitats. Of the 396 introduced and naturalised vascular plants on the Chathams, only 26 per cent occur in wetlands. Chathams wetlands are notable in another sense, too: although they have been much affected by fire, and grazing and trampling of livestock and wild mammals, they have been less affected by drainage and intensive agriculture, they do not receive the same degree of nutrient enrichment from agricultural fertilisers, and they lack most of the problematic weeds and introduced fish that have impacted upon mainland wetlands.

At least 23 of the 35 endemic Chatham Islands flowering plants and ferns occur in wetlands, and 10 of these are confined to wet sites. Notable examples are the shrubby Cox's matipo (*Myrsine coxii*), Chatham Island toetoe (*Cortaderia turbaria*), Chatham Island speargrass (*Aciphylla traversii*), and one of the many sedges, *Carex chathamica*.

Southern heaths (two species of *Dracophyllum*) were of particular importance as peat-formers. The endemic tarahinau (*D. arboreum*) is still the dominant tree of peatlands on the southern tablelands and on the uplands of Pitt Island. Its shrubby relative inaka (*D. scoparium*) is dominant in many north Chatham bogs and was once much more widespread across Chatham Island. The waxy leaves, hard wood and wiry roots of tarahinau and inaka are resistant to decay; all these plant parts contribute to the buildup of peat. Across much of the northern half of Chatham Island, peatlands that now have just a low vegetation of shrubs, ferns and sedges, nevertheless retain within the peat the buried root plates of long-dead and mainly fire-killed tarahinau and inaka.

Notable also as a peat-former is Chatham Island bamboo-rush (*Sporadanthus traversii*), which can grow to 3 metres tall, producing a dense tangle of branched wiry stems from a mass of thick underground stems (rhizomes). It is a dominant plant on the clears of the southern tablelands, and across gently sloping basins of northern Chatham, but

Vegetation in Te Awatea Scenic Reserve, showing plants typical of a fen. The leafless sedge is *Baumea rubiginosa*, and the fern is kiokio (*Blechnum novaezelandiae*). The cushion of *Sphagnum cristatum* has been cut to reveal the gradation from living stems, down to peat. The water table here is very close to ground level.

Peter Johnson

its vigour and extent continue to be affected by fire and cattle grazing. Bamboo-rush is oddly absent from Pitt Island.

Chatham Island bamboo-rush (*Sporadanthus traversii*).

Peter Johnson

All wetland plants contribute to peat formation, but special mention should also be made of sphagnum mosses, which are effective peat-formers worldwide. Typically growing as soft cushions, with their upper foliage alive and green, the lower stems gradually die but persist as fibrous peat. At least three species of *Sphagnum* grow on the Chathams, the common ones being the yellow-green cushion-forming *S. cristatum* that is common in open areas of bogs, and the more wispy and bright green *S. falcatulum*, which grows in shallow bog pools.

Not only is peat a result of wetland vegetation and processes, it also encourages further expansion and maintenance of wetland conditions. For example, peat can form upon dune sands or clay soils derived from volcanic rock, both of which are inherently well drained. The overlying peat promotes a process in the poorly aerated subsoil whereby iron materials solidify as an impervious hard layer that prevents downward drainage, and makes the peat even wetter. These iron pans can be readily seen in many roadside cuttings, resembling an old rusted sheet of iron and clearly separating the upper peat layer from the underlying and often friable sand or clay.

Over many thousands of years, deep accumulations of peat can create distinctive landforms. Blanket peat covers gently undulating land, hiding the topography beneath. Peat domes up to several hundred metres across grow upon gentle hill crests and spurs, with their deepest peat in the poorly drained centre and a prominent steep slope around their perimeter; Pitt Island has some good examples. When fully saturated, and therefore in their most heavy and best-lubricated state, large areas of peat can slump to form basins or hollows. Some peat lakes have resulted from this process, while lightning-induced or man-made fires, which can persist underground for many years, created others. A peat lake – one that is surrounded by peatland and probably also has a peat bed – usually has water that is stained deeply by both suspended and dissolved humus. A readily observed example is Kaipakau Lake, on the western side of Ocean Mail Scenic Reserve (misnamed Lake Wharemanu on some maps). On the southern tablelands, peat lakes such as Rakeinui are likewise very dark; as light does not penetrate far into the water, the main aquatic vegetation is of submerged mosses that can grow under conditions of heavy shade. All streams draining from peatlands are similarly brown-stained, and are also often lined with aquatic mosses, a feature that is helped by a general lack of scouring gravels or silt in the catchment.

Lakes of a very different nature occur in hollows behind sand dunes. Nestled behind the high dunes of Long Beach is a series of dune lakes, the largest being Marakapia, close to Chatham Lodge, and Tennants Lake, alongside Port Hutt Road. These lakes have a relatively constant water level, about 20 metres above sea level, and they all have clear fresh water, suitable for beds of aquatic vegetation, mainly milfoil (*Myriophyllum triphyllum*), stonewort algae (species of *Chara* and *Nitella*), and horse's mane weeds (*Ruppia megacarpa* and *R. polycarpa*). These are what the black swans feed on, especially in Te Whanga, where *Ruppia* can be seen as dark patches and bands from the air, or as piles of fine foliage storm-heaped along the shores. The aquatic plants are all native, and it is a remarkable fact that so far the freshwaters of the Chathams have not been invaded by the many troublesome aquatic weeds that occur through much of mainland New Zealand, such as oxygen weeds in the genera *Egeria*, *Elodea*, *Hydrilla* and *Lagarosiphon*.

Another chain of dune lakes lies along the eastern side of Te Whanga Lagoon, narrowly separated from the sea by a dune ridge (see page 145). These shallow freshwater lakes lie just above sea level and their roughly circular shapes suggest that they originated as 'pinched-off' former bays of Te Whanga. Each lake has its own characteristic colour, dependent on the amount of silt. Some have quite a stable water level, others like Lake Rangitai and its neighbours have a wider fluctuation, and this, combined with a very gently sloping shore, encourages distinctive zones of turf vegetation. Such zones are visible also in Ocean Mail Scenic Reserve, where North Road passes alongside several wet depressions. These are ephemeral wetlands, so called because they are not permanently wet, but

occupy hollows having no surface outlet, so that they pond during wet seasons and may dry out completely at the end of summer.

Turf wetlands are one of the botanical highlights of the Chathams, because they occur in many habitats and contain a multitude of different plants, all interlacing and growing no more than a few centimetres tall, like on a bowling green. In marshes beside tidal streams and on exposed coastal headlands the main plants are those tolerant of salt, such as

Dune lakes behind Long Beach in a view south over Petre Bay towards Red Bluff and Waitangi. Lake Te Roto (right), Tennants Lake (centre), and Lake Marakapia (left) are lakes of fresh, clear water containing aquatic vegetation that is still dominated by native plants.

Peter Johnson

An ephemeral wetland at Ocean Mail Scenic Reserve. Zones of vegetation include aquatic plants in the hollow, green turf, then rushlands. In the distance oioi (jointed wire rush, *Apodasmia similis*) stretches away towards Te Whanga Lagoon. The foreground clumps are knobby clubrush (*Ficinia nodosa*).

Peter Johnson

Turf vegetation growing on fibrous sandy peat, cut from the dune hollow behind Maunganui Beach. From left: remuremu (*Selliera radicans*; first two white flowers, fleshy leaves), sharp spike sedge (*Eleocharis acuta*; with erect stems), *Lobelia arenaria* (broad-toothed leaves, white starry flowers, purple fruit), and *Centella uniflora* (stalked, angled leaves).

Peter Johnson

glasswort (*Sarcocornia quinqueflora*), sea primrose (*Samolus repens*) and remuremu (*Selliera radicans*). These can all be readily seen on the shore at the Ohira basalt columns. A little further from the coast, numerous other plants join the turf. Behind Maunganui Beach, for example, within a very extensive dune hollow, a survey revealed 40 turf species, of which 27 were native. Although too many to list here, one is worthy of special mention. This is *Lobelia arenaria* (formerly *Pratia arenaria*), which also occurs in small populations on the Auckland Islands and on the southeast Otago coast, but it is most abundant on the Chathams. A creeping plant, with starry flowers (white or sometimes bluish) and purplish berries, it is a component of both coastal and inland turfs, as well as growing in bogs, on sand dunes, among long grass and under forest: a wetland plant that can grow anywhere!

Among the array of distinctive wetland types are the swamp forests, now much reduced in area because of agricultural development, and also much under-represented within protected areas. Many Chatham trees are capable of growing in swamps, notably karamu (*Coprosma chathamica*) and a variety of akeake (*Olearia traversii*), but also hoho (*Pseudopanax chathamicus*), matipo (*Myrsine chathamica*), and even nikau (*Rhopalostylis sapida*). Examples of swamp forest can still be seen close to Waitangi, such as near the south shore of Lake Huro, where cabbage trees (*Cordyline australis*) are conspicuous. Cabbage trees are believed to have been introduced from mainland New Zealand, and the similarly introduced tree fuchsia (*Fuchsia excorticata*), plus tutu (*Coriaria arborea*), also play a part in some swamp forests. Beneath the tree canopy typically there is a mixture of tree ferns and shrubs, tall *Carex* sedges, sometimes clumps of Moriori flax (*Astelia chathamica*), and a network of muddy puddles and partly hidden water channels.

Some wetlands have an appearance of uniformity and drabness when viewed from the outside, especially on a grey day. The numerous different sedges and rushes can appear quite similar to the untrained eye, and the prospect of getting wet and muddy can be a bit off-putting. Nevertheless, wetlands have their hidden charms, and those of the Chathams especially so. Flowers and fruits can be found at any time of year: little white bells upon the heath shrubs inaka and pouteretere (*Leptecophylla robusta*); purple flowers on sun orchids (*Thelymitra* spp.) and Chatham Island aster (*Olearia semidentata*); yellow flowers on silverweed (*Potentilla anserinoides*), bachelors button (*Cotula coronopifolia*) and little buttercups (*Ranunculus* spp.), not to mention the spectacular rautini (*Brachyglottis huntii*). Fleshy fruits on shrubby coprosmas range from cream to pinks and yellows, while those on pouteretere can be white, pink or red on different bushes. The flowers, of course, are really there for insects to be attracted for pollination duty, while the fruits are for birds to eat and spread the seeds.

Wetlands provide habitat for many plants, invertebrates, fish and birds, and are there for us to admire, appreciate, enjoy and look after. Maybe all those peatlands will be valued even more in the future, as sites that absorb atmospheric carbon dioxide and thus reduce humankind's impact on global climate.

Swamp forest at Mangape Creek, the outlet of Lake Huro. The main trees are Chatham Island karamu (*Coprosma chathamica*), swamp akeake (*Olearia* aff. *traversii*) and cabbage tree (*Cordyline australis*). The tall green sedgeland, in this case of *Carex ternaria*, occupies swampy flats that would formerly have had forest. In the foreground and at left upon drier parts of the flats are communities of tall rushes (*Juncus edgariae*), the shorter spike sedge (*Eleocharis acuta*) and introduced gorse (*Ulex europaeus*).

Peter Johnson

FRESHWATER FISH AND FROGS

The endemic Chatham Island mudfish (*Neochanna rekohua*), known only from lakes on the southern tablelands and their outlet streams, Chatham Island.

Tony Eldon

The Chatham Islands have a low diversity of native freshwater fish, with nine species on Chatham Island, and six of these also on Pitt Island. This contrasts with over 30 species of freshwater fish on mainland New Zealand. The only endemic freshwater fish is the Chatham Island mudfish (*Neochanna rekohua*), which is known from three lakes on southern Chatham Island. These populations are believed to be landlocked, but all other Chatham Island freshwater fish species are diadromous, meaning that they move between freshwater and the sea during their life cycle.

Diadromy enables fish to disperse throughout New Zealand and outlying islands such as the Chathams. Genetic research on the giant kokopu (*Galaxias argenteus*), banded kokopu (*Galaxias fasciatus*) and redfinned bully (*Gobiomorphus huttoni*) revealed that Chatham Island populations were genetically indistinguishable from mainland New Zealand fish. The Chatham Island mudfish is most closely related to the Canterbury mudfish (*Neochanna burrowsius*), which suggests a shared diadromous ancestor and a relatively recent dispersal from the mainland to the Chatham Islands.

Recreational harvest of freshwater fish on the Chathams is mostly limited to the harvest of eels, both the threatened longfinned eel (*Anguilla dieffenbachii*) and the shortfinned eel (*A. australis*), as well as whitebait and giant kokopu. The whitebait fishery is largely made up of common smelt (*Retropinna retropinna*) in Te Whanga Lagoon, with juveniles running in the spring, and adults later in summer. In contrast, the whitebait fishery on mainland New Zealand is mainly composed of juveniles of inanga (*Galaxias maculatus*) and other kokopu species. There is currently no commercial harvest of eels on the Chathams, although quota have been allocated for both species.

Chatham Island lakes and streams have very few introduced animals. Those present have apparently established following releases of aquarium pets. Goldfish (*Carassius auratus*) are found in a couple of private ponds on Chatham and Pitt Islands, and whistling frogs (*Litoria ewingii*) were recently found to be established inland from the Tuku Road south of Waitangi. There have also been unconfirmed reports of the larger southern bell frog (*L. raniformis*). Both these Australian frog species are widespread on mainland New Zealand. The effects of these introduced species on Chatham Island fish and insects are unknown, and care should be taken to prevent their further spread.

Nadine Bott

CHAPTER SEVEN

FLORA

The Chatham Islands are the easternmost extension of the New Zealand Botanical Region. About 650 kilometres from the mainland, they are remarkably isolated from other landmasses. Over the last 2.5 million years a distinctive flora has evolved, though it retains strong affinities with that of the rest of New Zealand.

The forests of the Chatham Islands are quite different from typical New Zealand forests. Low and windswept, the main canopy species belong to genera that elsewhere are typically shrubs. Many of the characteristic trees of New Zealand are absent, including podocarps (rimu, totara and allies) and southern beech trees (*Nothofagus* spp.). However, there are some that are identical to mainland populations, including silver fern (*Cyathea dealbata*), black tree fern (*C. medullaris*) and kawakawa (*Macropiper excelsum*). Some tree species were apparently introduced by Polynesians within the last 500 years, most notably kopi (karaka; *Corynocarpus laevigatus*), an important species in Moriori culture.

Unlike the grim litany of bird extinctions that have occurred since human settlement, no endemic Chatham Islands plant is known to have become extinct. However, many species are gravely threatened, with some dependent on conservation management to ensure their survival.

Baron Ferdinand von Mueller (1825–96) was a Melbourne-based botanist and author of *The Vegetation of the Chatham Islands* (1864), based on specimens collected by Henry Travers. This is still the only flora available for the Chatham Islands, and it laid the foundation for subsequent study and understanding of the islands' plants.

Royal Botanic Gardens, Melbourne

Above: **Chatham Island iceplant (*Disphyma papillatum*).** Helen Gummer

Relationships and characteristics of the flora

There are about 392 species, subspecies and varieties of flowering plant and fern that are considered indigenous to the Chatham Islands. A further 396 are regarded as naturalised (introduced and growing in the wild). Compared with the other outlying islands of the New Zealand archipelago (Kermadec Islands and the subantarctic islands), the Chatham Islands have the highest number of endemic plants. Some 34 flowering plant species, subspecies and varieties, and one fern are recognised as endemic to the islands, and at least a further 15 undescribed forms may also be endemic. Among the endemic species are the two monotypic genera *Embergeria* (Chatham Island sow thistle) and *Myosotidium* (Chatham Island forget-me-not).

While most Chathams plants are closely related to mainland New Zealand species, the relationships of the Chatham Island sow thistle and forget-me-not have proven difficult to resolve. Based on its DNA, the sow thistle is apparently allied to both the New Zealand endemic *Kirkianella* and the Australian endemic *Actites*. Outwardly the Chathams species has little obvious relationship to either, resembling rather a very large sow thistle or puha (*Sonchus* spp.). The relationship of *Myosotidium* to the rest of the forget-me-not family (Boraginaceae) is even more obscure, though it is known that it belongs to the tribe Cynoglosseae. This tribe includes the well-known and widely cultivated Chinese forget-me-not (*Cynoglossum amabile*).

The remaining Chathams plants have strong biogeographical links mainly to northern New Zealand, or to a lesser extent southern New Zealand and the subantarctic islands. Interestingly, many mosses and liverworts also show this pattern, as do the Chathams endemic seaweeds.

Below left: *Embergeria grandifolia*, the endemic sow thistle, once regarded as highly threatened, is now making a rapid recovery on fenced-off portions of the main islands. It is most easily seen on the shore around Kaingaroa.

Peter de Lange

Below right: The Chatham Island forget-me-not (*Myosotidium hortensia*) is probably the plant most readily identified with the islands, because it is so widely cultivated around the world.

Rod Morris, DOC

Left: **Keketerehe or Chatham Island tree-daisy (*Olearia chathamica*).**
Helen Gummer

Above: **The spectacular summer flowering of rautini (*Brachyglottis huntii*) provides the alternative name of Chatham Island Christmas tree.**
Peter de Lange

Below: **Chatham Island aster (*Olearia semidentata*, above) and keketerehe are now considered closely related to the subantarctic megaherb *Pleurophyllum speciosum* (below, photographed on Campbell Island).**
Geoff Davidson (above),
Colin Miskelly (below)

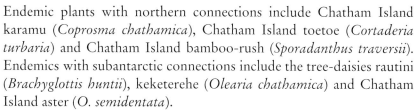

Endemic plants with northern connections include Chatham Island karamu (*Coprosma chathamica*), Chatham Island toetoe (*Cortaderia turbaria*) and Chatham Island bamboo-rush (*Sporadanthus traversii*). Endemics with subantarctic connections include the tree-daisies rautini (*Brachyglottis huntii*), keketerehe (*Olearia chathamica*) and Chatham Island aster (*O. semidentata*).

Rautini or Chatham Island Christmas tree is an icon. Recent DNA studies have shown that it is very closely related to *Brachyglottis stewartiae*, known from Foveaux Strait (Little Solander and the northern titi islands) and from the Snares Islands. Together these remarkable trees share a common ancestry with the eastern South Island subalpine shrub *B. cassinioides*.

Further molecular studies have confirmed that the large-flowered tree-daisies keketerehe and Chatham Island aster are more closely related to the subantarctic megaherbs *Pleurophyllum* and *Damnamenia* than they are to any of the other species of *Olearia*. It is likely that both species will soon be placed within *Pleurophyllum*. While at first this may seem far-fetched, the only real difference between *Pleurophyllum* and these *Olearia* species is the absence of a central trunk and branches.

Crystalwort (*Atriplex billardierei*) grows lower on the shoreline than any other native flowering plant. This species is now extinct in the South and Stewart Islands, and is threatened in Australia, where it now known only from Tasmania.

Colin Miskelly

An Australian–Chathams connection evident in one flowering plant (*Leucopogon parviflorus*) also has parallels among the liverwort and moss flora. The Australian connection is further strengthened if one includes two Australian coastal strand plants, *Atriplex australasica* and crystalwort (*A. billardierei*), both of which were always scarce and are now apparently extinct from the rest of New Zealand but remain abundant on the Chatham Islands. Chatham Island populations of the coastal cress *Lepidium flexicaule* also are more like those from Australia than mainland New Zealand.

An ongoing nationwide study of Cook's scurvy grass (*Lepidium oleraceum*) has revealed that Chatham Islands populations may be derived from multiple dispersal events from New Zealand, with consequent varying levels of divergence. Some Chatham Islands populations have DNA sequences identical to plants from northern New Zealand, while others possess sequences unique to the Chatham Islands.

A peculiarity of the shared New Zealand–Chatham Islands flora is the large number of plants known from only one or two populations on the islands, and in some extreme cases from only one or two individuals. This pattern has led researchers to speculate on whether these plants are indigenous. Raupo (*Typha orientalis*), for example, is restricted to a single site on Chatham Island, adjacent to a former Maori occupation site. Raupo was used by Maori for food and medicine (rongoa), and there is an oral tradition that it was brought to the island. Similarly, DNA sequence data from cabbage trees (*Cordyline australis*) on Chatham Island match plants from northern Taranaki,

Three possibly distinct forms of Cook's scurvy grass (*Lepidium oleraceum*) are known from the Chatham Islands. The most threatened of these has its main population at Kaingaroa.

Peter de Lange

Hoho (*Pseudopanax chathamicus*), the endemic species of lancewood, has no juvenile phase and the adult foliage is much broader than its mainland relative horoeka (*P. crassifolius*).

Colin Miskelly

suggesting that these, too, were brought to the islands by Ngati Mutunga and Ngati Tama. Further DNA research may also resolve the provenance of kopi, kowhai (*Sophora chathamica*) and a range of sedges, ferns and shrubs that have distributions perhaps best explained by human intervention.

Another intriguing feature of the Chatham Islands is the near absence of plants with a divaricating growth habit (including wiry interlacing stems and small leaves). For example, many mainland species of *Coprosma* and *Corokia* are divaricating, while only one Chatham Island species is (*Coprosma propinqua* var. *propinqua*, which is also present throughout mainland New Zealand). Similarly, hoho (*Pseudopanax chathamicus*) is very closely related to the New Zealand lancewood (*P. crassifolius*), yet hoho does not have the distinct juvenile growth phase so familiar to New Zealand gardeners. The same is true of Chatham Island ribbonwood (*Plagianthus regius* subsp. *chathamicus*), whose only claim to separate status from the New Zealand ribbonwood (*P. regius* subsp. *regius*) is the lack of a juvenile divaricating growth phase.

Both Chatham speargrasses (*Aciphylla dieffenbachii* and *A. traversii*) differ from their New Zealand relatives by having softer, floppy leaves, though both retain sharp leaf tips. Indeed, the only spiny native plant on the Chatham Islands is matagouri (*Discaria toumatou*), which is scarce there, and so is perhaps a recent arrival or accidental import.

Ecologists have long pondered the near absence of divaricating and juvenile forms and reduction in spiny leaves, all of which are features of the plants of New Zealand's offshore islands. Some suggest that

Coxella (*Aciphylla dieffenbachii*) has much softer foliage than its fearsome mainland speargrass relatives.

Peter de Lange

these differences are climate-induced, noting that all of these growth habits and leaf modifications are common adaptations seen in alpine and dryland plants, and are redundant on moist, temperate islands. Yet others argue that the absences are proof of the role moa played in the evolution of plant defence mechanisms on mainland New Zealand, a hypothesis supported by the absence of moa on the Chatham Islands.

Trees

The forest vegetation is dominated by only a few, mostly endemic tree species. The tallest is the nikau palm (*Rhopalostylis sapida*), which is sometimes considered distinct from the mainland species. The Pitt Island populations of nikau, known locally as 'cabbage trees', have the distinction of being the southernmost palms in the world.

Chatham Island akeake (*Olearia traversii*) was the predominant coastal tree on the Chatham Islands on better-drained soils and stable sand dunes, but cannot regenerate in the presence of farm stock.

Kate McAlpine

Chatham Island akeake (*Olearia traversii*) is the dominant tree species on sand dunes and better-drained soils. Not to be confused with the globally widespread *Dodonaea viscosa*, known in New Zealand as akeake, the quite unrelated Chatham Island akeake is by far the tallest *Olearia* species. Chatham Island akeake produces durable timber, used for fenceposts and firewood. When dry, the wood burns with much heat, and produces little ash and smoke. So it can truly be said that Chatham Islanders use daisies for firewood! Regrettably there are now very few places where akeake dune forest remains intact. However, akeake has been planted at several restoration sites, including Ocean Mail Scenic Reserve on the Tioriori coast, and most notably on Mangere Island. It is also regenerating well on fenced dunelands.

In more sheltered sites forest dominated by Chatham Island matipo (*Myrsine chathamica*) and Chatham Island karamu is common. Both species are among the largest known from their respective genera. While the karamu is endemic, the matipo is shared with a few islands in Foveaux Strait. Kopi stands are also common near the coast, and in places these have replaced or merged with the matipo/karamu forest. Kopi was probably introduced to the Chatham Islands by Moriori, who ate its fruit and carved rakau momori on the living trunks.

Inland on deeper peat soils tarahinau (*Dracophyllum arboreum*) and pouteretere (*Leptecophylla robusta*) are prominent. As with akeake, karamu and matipo, these species are also the largest of their respective genera. Tarahinau trees up to 18 metres tall are known, while 8-metre-tall pouteretere are common in some of the southern tablelands forests. Associated with these forests and along river valleys is another giant, Barker's koromiko (*Hebe barkeri*). Reaching heights of 8–10 metres, this is the world's tallest hebe.

In extremely wet sites a distinctive swamp forest is dominated by karamu, matipo, swamp karamu (*Coprosma propinqua* var. *martinii*) and an as-yet-unnamed variant of *Olearia traversii*. This forest typically forms

Barker's koromiko (*Hebe barkeri*)
the world's tallest hebe.

over areas of almost permanently flooded ground, or on the margins of slowly flowing creeks and rivers, making it difficult to investigate. It was only in 2007 that botanists recognised the distinctiveness of the swamp forest akeake, which was a surprise to those islanders who had long known that the 'shell akeake' was distinct from the more widespread form of akeake. Botanists still have a lot to learn from island residents.

Plants of the coastline

Most shore habitats now have many introduced plants, such as marram grass (*Ammophila arenaria*), purple ragwort (*Senecio elegans*) and horned poppy (*Glaucium flavum*). However, New Zealand spinach (*Tetragonia tetragonioides*), Chatham Island forget-me-not, Chatham Island sow thistle, shore dock (*Rumex neglectus*) and nettle (*Urtica australis*) may be present, and are locally dominant in places, such as at Kaingaroa. At least one unnamed endemic scurvy grass is also known from here, though the same plant also grows around petrel burrows on Rabbit Island, and among Chatham Island button-daisy (*Leptinella*

Poor Knights spleenwort
(*Asplenium pauperequitum*) at
Point Somes: a fern only recently
recognised as occurring on the
Chatham Islands.

John Sawyer

featherstonii) on the jagged cliff faces of the Forty Fours.

The smaller islands and rock stacks are the typical home of this unusual button-daisy. While the other New Zealand button-daisies tend to be small, creeping or tufted herbs, *L. featherstonii* is a woody shrub up to one metre tall (see page 82). It is the dominant flowering plant on many outlying islands, a marked contrast to its near-extinct status on the main islands. Usually associated with the button-daisy is *Senecio radiolatus* subsp. *radiolatus*, another Chatham Island endemic, and one with a high requirement for guano. It is now scarce in the main islands, though it still flourishes near seabird roosts and on exposures of guano-rich soils along the northwestern coastline. Another as-yet-unnamed scurvy grass also has its stronghold on the outer islands. This form of scurvy grass is also known from the Antipodes Islands, where it is very uncommon.

On some northern schist outcrops and the Forty Fours the Poor Knights spleenwort (*Asplenium pauperequitum*) is present. This fern was considered to be an endangered local endemic of the Poor Knights Islands off northern New Zealand, until its discovery on the Chatham Islands in 2005. However, the most common fern of coastal sites is the endemic Chatham Island spleenwort (*A. chathamense*).

The spectacular coxella (*Aciphylla dieffenbachii*) is very susceptible to browsing by sheep, and is now confined to cliff faces and offshore islands. At these sites it often occurs among extensive swards of Chatham Island iceplant (*Disphyma papillatum*). This iceplant has both

pink- and white-flowered forms that create an impressive summer show at protected sites. The purple flowers of the prostrate Chatham Island koromiko (*Hebe chathamica*) add to the floral effect.

Wetland plants

The peat bogs of Chatham Island are dominated by Chatham Island bamboo-rush (*Sporadanthus traversii*), with lesser amounts of the spectacular purple-flowered Chatham Island aster and white-flowered inaka (*Dracophyllum scoparium*). These peat-bog systems are unique to the Chatham Islands, and contain many interesting plant species. Chatham Island speargrass (*Aciphylla traversii*) is at times prominent, as is the shrubby Cox's matipo (*Myrsine coxii*), the latter especially around forest–wetland margins. *Sporadanthus* itself is another Chathams specialty, though anyone who has struggled through its dense bamboo-like thickets is unlikely to appreciate its significance. The genus was originally described from the Chatham Islands, but related species are now known from the northern North Island, and eastern Australia and Tasmania.

Hebe chathamica, one of the three endemic species of koromiko.
Mike Wilcox

Weeds

Until recently little attention had been paid to surveying or controlling weeds on the Chatham Islands. However, a major programme of gorse (*Ulex europaeus*) control is now under way, and the Department of Conservation has attempted to eradicate or contain several environmental weed species.

The Chatham Islands have a weed flora that is a subset of, and derived largely from, the New Zealand weed flora. Although half of the known flowering plants on the islands are non-native, the Chatham Islands are still remarkably weed-free. This may be one reason why using fences to exclude browsing animals from indigenous vegetation has been

Chilean guava (*Ugni molinae*), known locally as cranberry, is one of the most insidious weeds on the Chathams. Introduced as a garden plant, it is dispersed by birds and cattle, and now covers hundreds of hectares of northern Chatham Island, where its low growth form blends in with the native ferns and shrubs.

Peter Johnson

Garden plants that have escaped near Flower Pot, Pitt Island. Gardens now pose one of the main ways in which introduced plants become established on the islands.

Peter de Lange

such a successful conservation strategy on the islands. This contrasts with mainland New Zealand, where reducing browsing pressure often results in a proliferation of weeds.

A peculiarity of the Chatham Islands flora has been the naturalisation of indigenous mainland New Zealand plants on the islands. In some cases this has had a serious impact on the island. Taupata (*Coprosma repens*), for example, now dominates the coastal cliffs, headlands and rocky beaches of all the main settlements. It is only a matter of time before it colonises the more remote islands and islets, to the detriment of their flora and any dependent fauna. Further, taupata will probably hybridise with endemic Chatham *Coprosma* species. This has already happened with its close relative, the (also introduced) New Zealand karamu (*C. robusta*), which forms an extensive hybrid swarm with both Chatham Island karamu and swamp karamu along the Owenga Road.

Hybridism between close New Zealand–Chatham relatives is a serious threat to the indigenous flora of the Chatham Islands. In addition to the existing *Coprosma* situation, rangiora (*Brachyglottis repanda*) will hybridise with rautini (*B. huntii*) in cultivation. It is only a matter of time before this happens on the Chathams, and the impacts on rautini could be devastating. Other potentially troublesome New Zealand natives slowly spreading on the islands include karo (*Pittosporum crassifolium*) and pohutukawa (*Metrosideros excelsa*).

Most weed species reached the Chatham Islands as deliberately introduced garden plants. Many of these 'escaped' from cultivation, and this ongoing process is readily seen around all the settlements on the islands. While some species may fail to thrive in unmodified habitats, it is likely that there are many costly environmental timebombs ticking among currently innocuous escapees.

Plant conservation

The Chatham Islands are home to a highly threatened flora, with 22 per cent of the endemic flowering plants and ferns listed as 'Threatened' or 'At Risk'. This figure includes such well-known icons as rautini, Chatham Island forget-me-not and Chatham Island akeake. Several Chatham Islands species, including at least one unnamed endemic scurvy grass, are perilously close to extinction.

The major success story of Chatham Islands plant conservation over the past 20 years has been the large number of landowners who have made a commitment to protecting remnant forests and other special corners of their farms. Regeneration rates are spectacular, but some vulnerable species require more assistance than just fencing out farm stock, or possum control. This has included specialist techniques such as DNA fingerprinting to determine genetic variation in remnant populations, carefully monitored propagation trials, and surveys of key

The Department of Conservation
restoration plant nursery at
Te One.

Peter Moore

habitats likely to hold unreported populations of threatened species. Species that have benefited from this work include Chatham Island toetoe, scurvy grasses and Chatham Island forget-me-not.

A few species, notably Moriori flax (*Astelia chathamica*), Chatham Island speargrass, Chatham Island sow thistle and Chatham Island ribbonwood, have responded so well to management that they have been afforded the rare distinction of being ranked as 'Recovering' under the New Zealand threat-ranking classification.

While there are good stories to tell about the recovery of the Chatham Islands flora, there have also been significant failures. Despite ongoing management, at least two endemic plants are still declining. While hundreds of rautini still exist, seedlings are scarce, and there are indications that some populations are afflicted with an as-yet-unidentified fungal pathogen. To make matters worse, adults and juveniles are targeted by possums, and there is some suggestion that plants are 'self-incompatible'. This means that mature plants need to be fertilised by unrelated plants in order to set viable seed. Isolated plants, or plantings derived from a single remnant population, may never be able to reproduce. A similar situation appears to hold for Barker's koromiko. Clearly, for these species at least, we have much more to learn before we can truly call them secure from extinction.

There is still much work to be done to protect the threatened plants and plant communities of the Chatham Islands – from the threat of stock, wild pigs, possums and competition from naturalised plants. However, the work done so far is of great importance for the survival of the flora of this remote botanic outpost.

MOSSES

About 170 moss species are known from the Chatham Islands, only one of which (*Macromitrium ramsayae*) is endemic. Perhaps five species are naturalised, with the remainder native to New Zealand, Australasia or the wider Pacific. The majority are widespread species found throughout the main islands of New Zealand.

Several Chatham Islands mosses have interesting biogeographical affinities. *Macromitrium brevicaule* occurs elsewhere on offshore islands and coastal headlands from Coromandel Peninsula to Northland. The nationally endangered and distinctive *Archidium elatum* is elsewhere known only from Ahipara (where it may be extinct), Moturoa Island, and the nearby Black Rocks, all in Northland. Of the 18 species of *Fissidens* known from the Chathams, one (*Fissidens oblongifolius* var. *oblongifolius*) is an uncommon species also known from Northland south to Rangitoto Island. Another (*F. oblongifolius* var. *hyophilus*) also has a northern New Zealand distribution, apart from disjunct Wellington and Kaikoura populations.

Chathams mosses with southern connections include the aquatic *Blindia immersa*, elsewhere known from western South Island, Stewart Island and the Auckland Islands; and *Muelleriella crassifolia*, a salt-tolerant coastal species shared with Otago as well as Stewart, Snares, Auckland, Campbell and Macquarie Islands, southern South America and parts of Antarctica.

Two recent Chatham discoveries belong to the tropical family Calymperaceae. *Calymperes tenerum* is widespread in the Pacific, Southeast Asia and northern Australia and also occurs at scattered western hemisphere tropical localities. In Polynesia it is most commonly found on the

The endemic moss *Macromitrium ramsayae* is common, forming dense velvety mats on coastal tree trunks and rock outcrops.

Peter de Lange & Jeremy Rolfe

The tropical moss *Calymperes tenerum* reaches its southern-most limit on the Chatham Islands. This moss is rarely fertile, reproducing mainly by the small pompom-shaped brood bodies produced at the tips of the leaves.

Bill Malcolm

trunks of coconut palms or on coconut husks. It has been found growing on bark of karamu and nikau on Chatham and Pitt Islands. The related *Syrrhopodon armatus* is widespread in the African and Asian tropics and in Australia. In the Chathams it is known from Rabbit Island and the head of Wairarapa Creek. Elsewhere in New Zealand it is recorded only from the Kermadec and Poor Knights Islands, and from a few places in eastern Northland and the Coromandel Peninsula.

Five of the six introduced moss species are not generally considered a threat to Chatham species. However, an attempt has been made to eradicate the sixth, *Fissidens taxifolius*, from the single recorded Chatham Island site at Te One.

Allan Fife & Peter de Lange

Fissidens taxifolius, an aggressive weedy moss from the Northern Hemisphere, was discovered on Chatham Island in 2006. Never fertile in New Zealand, this species is spread in potting mix and garden waste.

Bill Malcolm

LIVERWORTS AND HORNWORTS

Currently 262 liverworts and nine hornwort species are known from the Chatham Islands, although none is endemic. The absence of endemic liverworts is intriguing and unexpected, possibly explained by the effective long-distance dispersal mechanisms of liverworts. However, further searching may yet reveal endemic species.

Compared with the rest of New Zealand, liverworts are not a prominent component of Chatham Islands vegetation. There are many species, but few are widespread and common. Many factors could be responsible, but land clearance and dry summer conditions are likely to be the main ones. Nevertheless, some distinctive liverwort-dominated vegetation types exist, especially within bamboo-rush bogs, and in poorly drained, reverting pasture. These 'liverwort turfs' are dominated by one or two species of *Riccardia*, and are usually rich emerald green, sometimes darkening to red following frost. Other sites with dense liverwort communities include forested ravines and shaded stream sides in the southern tablelands.

The diminutive liverwort *Archeophylla schusteri* is most abundant on the New Zealand subantarctic islands.

John Braggins

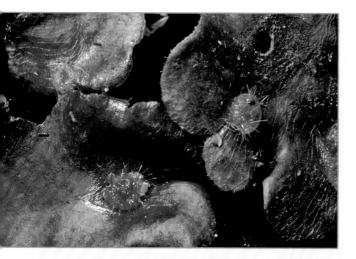

The liverwort *Dumortiera hirsuta* reaches its southernmost limit on the Chatham Islands.

John Braggins

The weedy *Marchantia polymorpha* was discovered on Chatham Island in 2006, and probably arrived as a contaminant in nursery plants. If left unchecked it rapidly smothers seedlings, but it typically does not thrive in natural habitats.

Peter de Lange

As with the flowering plants, ferns and mosses, the Chathams liverworts have three distinctive biogeographical relationships: with northern or southern New Zealand, or with Australia. The predominant group is species typical of, or known only from northern New Zealand, some of which reach their southern limits on the Chatham Islands. Two species (*Plagiochila fuscella* and *Archeophylla schusteri*) reveal a subantarctic connection. A further two (*Kurzia dendroides* and *Lopholejeunea muelleriana* var. *muelleriana*) are shared with Australia and have yet to be found on mainland New Zealand. The rest of the liverwort flora comprises mainly lowland species that are widespread and common throughout New Zealand.

Threatened liverworts on the Chatham Islands include the tropical *Dumortiera hirsuta*. While widespread overseas, in New Zealand it has been recorded only from a few northern sites and is regarded as nationally critical. The aquatic *Ricciocarpos natans* is another threatened species. It grows only in still or very slowly flowing, moderately fertile water and so far is known only from two sites on Chatham Island, where it is scarce.

A surprising recent discovery was *Plagiochila bazzanioides*, elsewhere known only from Rangitoto Island, and the Paparoa Range in north Westland. This serves as a reminder that with such poorly known groups as liverworts we are not yet sure of their true distributions.

David Glenny & Peter de Lange

LICHENS

Lichens were probably among the first colonists of the newly emerged Chatham Islands. Arriving as small wind-borne propagules, they were able to grow in the harshest of habitats, including coastal rocks, where lichens are still prominent today.

Lichens are not strictly plants, but rather a partnership (symbiosis) between two or more different organisms: a fungus providing the lichen body, and an enclosed photosynthetic partner which is either an alga or a cyanobacterium. Lichens are slow growing and long lived. They absorb moisture and nutrients from rainfall, mist or dew, and are capable of surviving in a dried state.

It is likely that several hundred types of lichen occur on the Chathams, given that over 1750 are known from New Zealand generally. Over 200 species have so far been collected on the islands. Their range of attractive colours is matched by their variety of growth forms. Crustose lichens adhere closely to rock or bark. Fruticose lichens are branched like tiny shrubs, such as the greyish *Stereocaulon* found on roadside banks.

Foliose lichens are leaf-like and may grow to hand-sized sheets, as do the several species of Pseudocyphellaria decorating tree trunks in tarahinau forests. Some of the smallest lichens grow upon the leaves of trees and shrubs. Look closely at the older leaves of hoho in Nikau Bush Conservation Area and you will see that they are miniature lichen gardens.

Diverse lichens growing on keketerehe bark near Rangaika, including the fruticose old man's beard lichen (*Usnea articulata*, upper left), and three foliose *Pseudocyphellaria* species (*P. coronata*, *P. granulata* and *P. rubella*).
Colin Miskelly

Crustose lichens on schist rocks near Te Whakaru Island, Chatham Island. A zone of yellow lichens (mainly *Caloplaca*) lies just above the uppermost tide level, while the upper rocks have a zone of *Pertusaria* looking like splashes of matt white paint.

Peter Johnson

Coral lichens (*Cladia* spp.) are the characteristic lichens of Chatham peatlands. These grow on the ground as white or yellowish masses, soft and spongy when wet, yet harsh and brittle when dry. On a smaller scale, many different pixie-cup lichens (*Cladonia*) grow on peat surfaces bared by fire or disturbance. Usually grey-green, they are sometimes adorned with brilliant red sporing organs.

Most coastal rocks are well decorated with lichens. At the Ohira basalt columns and on the schist rocks at Kaingaroa, lichens form distinctive zones of contrasting colours. A black lichen (*Verrucaria*) covers intertidal rocks, grading upslope to a yellow zone of *Caloplaca* and *Xanthoria*, then a prominent white zone, made up mainly of *Pertusaria*. Where it is more sheltered and less salty, larger grey and green lichens cover the upper rocks and extend onto the bark of akeake trunks.

The crumbly coastal slopes of Red Bluff Tuff near Waitangi support few lichens. However, a recent collection of a yellow shore lichen near the wharf turned out to be a new species. Now named *Caloplaca maculata*, and not known so far from anywhere else, it provides an indication that further lichens probably await discovery on the Chathams. This may be especially so upon Chathams limestones, for calcareous rocks typically support a distinctive lichen flora.

Peter Johnson

FUNGI

Around 300 fungal species have been recorded from the Chatham Islands, and many more, especially native species, await discovery and description. At least eight endemic fungi are known, including several undescribed forms. Most species are shared with mainland New Zealand, and about half are naturalised (i.e. not native). A striking feature compared to the mainland is the scarcity of conspicuous large species, due to the absence of key host trees such as beeches and tea-trees. However, a few large naturalised species, including the spectacular fly agaric (*Amanita muscaria*), grow under planted pine trees.

Although the dearth of large forest trees limits fungal diversity, large mushrooms and bracket fungi that grow on dead or diseased wood are better represented on the Chathams. Examples include the edible oyster mushroom (*Pleurotus*) and ear fungus (*Auricularia cornea*), often present on kopi.

The true diversity of Chatham fungi is revealed among the microfungi, especially those that infect living plant tissue. One of the most striking of these is the threatened rust fungus *Puccinia embergeria*, known only from the Kaingaroa population of the Chatham Island sow thistle. An undescribed rust fungus was recently found on nursery-grown Chatham Island forget-me-nots, but has not yet been found in the wild. Conservation of these rare rusts needs to be considered when their nearly-as-rare hosts are being propagated for restoration plantings.

Other Chathams endemic microfungi include one that causes tar-spot lesions on leaves of Chatham Island matipo, and three host-specific *Mycosphaerella* species that cause leaf spots on Chatham Island karamu, Chatham Island mahoe (*Melicytus chathamicus*), and keketerehe respectively.

Several Chatham Islands fungi are shared with the subantarctic islands, including the rusts *Puccinia chathamica* and *P. kirkii*, four species of Xylariaceae, and the small, bright blue-green wood-inhabiting mushroom *Mycena austrororida*. Similarities between the fungal biota of the Chathams and the subantarctic islands are probably due to their similar climates and plant communities, coupled with the great dispersal ability of most fungi.

Peter Johnston & Ross Beever

Oyster mushroom (*Pleurotus* sp.) growing on kopi (*Corynocarpus laevigatus*).
Ross Beever

The highly threatened endemic rust fungus (*Puccinia embergeria*) is known only from Chatham Island sow thistle at Kaingaroa, where it grows on just a few host plants. It is visible only while fruiting, when the fruits form orange lesions on the underside of the sow thistle leaves.
Peter de Lange

Table 1. Endemic plants of the Chatham Islands

Ferns

Asplenium chathamense — Chatham Island spleenwort

Trees & shrubs

Brachyglottis huntii — rautini
Coprosma chathamica — Chatham Island karamu
Coprosma propinqua var. *martinii* — swamp karamu, Chatham Island mingimingi
Corokia macrocarpa — hokataka, Chatham Island korokio
Dracophyllum arboreum — tarahinau
Hebe barkeri — Barker's koromiko
Hebe chathamica — Chatham Island koromiko
Hebe dieffenbachii — Dieffenbach's koromiko
Leptecophylla robusta — pouteretere
Melicytus chathamicus — Chatham Island mahoe
Myrsine coxii — Cox's matipo, swamp matipo
Olearia chathamica — keketerehe
Olearia semidentata — Chatham Island aster, swamp aster
Olearia traversii — Chatham Island akeake
Plagianthus regius subsp. *chathamicus* — Chatham Island ribbonwood
Pseudopanax chathamicus — hoho, Chatham Island lancewood

Grasses

Cortaderia turbaria — Chatham Island toetoe
Festuca coxii — Cox's fescue
Poa chathamica — Chatham Island poa

Sedges & rush-like plants

Carex chathamica — Chatham Island swamp sedge
Carex ventosa — Chatham Island forest sedge
Sporadanthus traversii — Chatham Island bamboo-rush

Orchids

Pterostylis silvicultrix — Chatham Island greenhood, tutukiwi

Herbs

Aciphylla dieffenbachii — coxella, Dieffenbach's speargrass, soft speargrass
Aciphylla traversii — Chatham Island speargrass
Astelia chathamica — Moriori flax, Chatham Island kakaha
Callitriche petriei subsp. *chathamensis* — Chatham Island starwort
Disphyma papillatum — Chatham Island iceplant
Embergeria grandifolia — Chatham Island sow thistle
Gentianella chathamica — Chatham Island gentian
Geranium traversii — Chatham Island geranium
Leptinella featherstonii — Chatham Island button-daisy
Myosotidium hortensia — Chatham Island forget-me-not
Senecio radiolatus subsp. *radiolatus* — Chatham Island groundsel

Mosses

Macromitrium ramsayae

(continued)

Endemic plants (continued)	
Seaweeds	
Carpococcus linearis	
Ceramium chathamense	
Durvillaea chathamensis	Chatham Island bull kelp
Gigartina grandifida	
Landsburgia myricifolia	
Lessonia tholiformis	
Pyrophyllon cameronii	
Lichens	
Caloplaca maculata	
Fungi	
Chalara distans	saprobe on tarahinau
Chalara dracophylli	saprobe on tarahinau
Circinotrichum chathamiensis	saprobe on Chatham Island matipo
Phyllachora hauturu ssp. *rekohu*	leaf spot on Chatham Island matipo
Puccinia embergeriae	embergeria rust

Table 2. New Zealand native plants naturalised on the Chatham Islands

Trees & shrubs	
Brachyglottis compacta × *B. greyi*	
Brachyglottis repanda	rangiora
Coprosma repens	taupata
Coprosma robusta	New Zealand karamu
Cordyline australis	cabbage tree, ti kouka
Corynocarpus laevigatus	kopi, karaka
Dodonaea viscosa	akeake
Fuchsia excorticata	tree fuchsia, kotukutuku
Hebe elliptica	kokomuka
Hoheria populnea	lacebark, houhere
Leptospermum scoparium	kahikatoa, manuka
Metrosideros excelsa	pohutukawa
Myoporum laetum	ngaio
Pittosporum crassifolium	karo
Sophora chathamica	coastal kowhai
Vines	
Clematis paniculata	puawhanga, New Zealand clematis
Grasses	
Poa cita	silver tussock
Rushes	
Juncus pallidus	
Herbs	
Arthropodium cirratum	rengarenga lily
Phormium tenax	New Zealand harakeke, flax

CHAPTER EIGHT

TERRESTRIAL INVERTEBRATES

One of the finest natural features of the Chatham Islands is the abundance of large ground-dwelling insects found in the forested areas of Rangatira Island. On a warm summer night, beneath flocks of returning petrels, thousands of insects swarm. There are weta climbing in trees and, on the forest floor, Chatham Island cockroaches (*Celatoblatta brunni*) are everywhere, together with hundreds of darkling beetles (*Mimopeus* spp.), dozens of Chatham Island stag beetles (*Geodorcus capito*) and large, predatory ground beetles (*Mecodema alternans*). Rather less common, Chatham Island click beetles (*Amychus candezei*) crawl over tree trunks.

By contrast, on the inhabited islands of the Chathams – or indeed of mainland New Zealand in similar lowland conditions – night observation reveals only a few cockroaches, the occasional weta and a variety of small beetles. Night viewing of insects on Rangatira Island gives one an idea of what much of lowland New Zealand was like before the arrival of people and their highly destructive fellow travellers, especially rats.

There are over 800 insect species on the Chatham Islands – around 8 per cent of the described New Zealand insect fauna. One out of every four or five species is endemic. But many prominent mainland insect groups, including stoneflies and blackflies (sandflies), do not occur on the Chathams. Some members of plant-eating groups that feed only on relatives of karamu, hoho or inaka are absent, despite the presence of

Top: Female (left) and male Chatham Island stag beetles (*Geodorcus capito*). John Marris

suitable habitats or hosts. There are conflicting interpretations of this enigma and no satisfactory explanation.

The present impoverished fauna on Chatham and Pitt Islands results from the large-scale clearing of native vegetation and the introduction of sheep, cattle, pigs, possums, rats, mice, cats, hedgehogs and weka. Much of the insect fauna still survives, although most of the large, flightless, endemic species are restricted to islands free of rodents and weka. And insect pest species from mainland New Zealand are becoming increasingly common.

The Chatham Islands are an excellent outdoor laboratory in which to test ideas on biogeography – the study of the distribution of plants and animals. One part of the fauna, of mostly endemic species, suggests a land connection with New Zealand, as they and all their relatives are flightless or poorly flighted. These endemics include the large Chatham Island stag beetle and click beetle, the Pitt Island longhorn, the coxella weevil, and a litter moth (Oecophoridae, unnamed). However, geologists now believe that the land that makes up the Chatham Islands re-emerged from the sea only about 2.5 million years ago, and that there has been no subsequent land bridge to the mainland. This means that even the flightless, endemic species must have reached the Chathams over the sea, perhaps on logs or rafts of debris swept out of rivers in major floods. Species of a second, more mobile group (for example the Chatham Island red admiral butterfly) are also endemic or have a distinctive Chathams form, indicating present isolation. The endemic species co-exist with species indistinguishable from those on the mainland, whose presence on the Chathams implies contemporary over-sea dispersal. Therefore, it seems that while some species reach the Chatham Islands very infrequently, others disperse regularly to the islands.

The predator-free southern islands of the Chathams support huge populations of the weta species *Talitropsis megatibia* (left) and *Novoplectron serratum* (below). These insects supplement their usual vegetarian diet with flesh from the carcasses of dead seabirds.

John Marris

The endemic Chatham Island cicada (*Kikihia longula*) is the only cicada known from the islands, where it is common. The grey foliose lichen is *Parmotrema crinitum*, growing on tarahinau.

Colin Miskelly

Male Chatham Island stag beetles (*Geodorcus capito*) have large mandibles, which they use in jousting battles against rivals.

John Marris

Some insect groups are in need of further study, for example blowflies. The Pitt Island blowfly (*Xenocalliphora solitaria*) is known from only one specimen but it probably has a wider distribution.

Among the more conspicuous insect groups the aquatics (particularly those of lakes and slow-moving streams) are represented by few species but hordes of individuals; for example, chironomid midges (12 species), caddisflies (six) and mosquitoes (now three, alas!). In sheltered openings the ranger dragonfly (*Procordulia smithii*), the blue damselfly (*Austrolestes colensoni*) and redcoat damselflies (*Xanthocnemis tuanuii* and *X. zealandica*) are abundant, while the Chatham Island cicada (*Kikihia longula*) sings on warm summer days. On the coast, kelp flies (four species) are numerous, and the large, pallid endemic rove beetle (*Thinocafius insularis*) and the seashore earwig (*Anisolabis litorea*) are common under seaweed.

In the forest and around houses three cave weta (Rhaphidophoridae) are found: the stout-legged *Talitropsis* spp. and the slender *Novoplectron serratum*. On Rangatira Island they rapidly dispose of the carcasses of petrels that have died while crashing through the canopy.

On the larger islands dead kopi logs are tunnelled by grubs of the orange-fawn longhorn *Xuthodes punctipennis*, and any dead tree or fallen branch will be pocked with circular holes, sure evidence of pit weevils (*Psepholax* spp. and the longer-legged *Strongylopterus chathamensis*).

Old logs and decaying branches are infested with two small stag beetles, one of which, *Mitophyllus reflexus*, is endemic.

South of the Tuku Valley, on Pitt Island and on some of the smaller islands large stag beetles (*Geodorcus* spp.) can still be found. Spiky caterpillars of the endemic subspecies *ida* of the red admiral butterfly feed only on the nettle *Urtica australis*, which often grows in drifts around sheds and forest margins. Nettles are also browsed (as are ribbonwood leaves) by wiggly green caterpillars of an endemic deltoid moth, *Udea pantheropa*. As you brush through the forest the stout caterpillar of the mahoe moth (*Homohadena fortis*) may land on you. It is brightly marked and distasteful to birds unless they can strip out the gut. Or you might encounter the striped caterpillar of the forest looper (*Pseudocoremia ombrodes*), which feeds on nearly all trees and shrubs (except karamu). On karamu, the bumpy brown looper caterpillar (*Austrocidaria simulata*) imitates dead twigs, and the bright green caterpillar of the endemic *A. haemophaea* imitates parts of a leaf.

A red admiral butterfly (*Vanessa gonerilla ida*) on a Chatham Island forget-me-not flower. The caterpillars feed on the nettle *Urtica australis* (foreground).

Helen Gummer

In open country (the 'clears') more insect life is found in the tangle fern/sphagnum/inaka community. Most species are day-active as adults, with distinctive but small species living on tangle fern (the tangle fern leafroller, *Ericodesma* spp.), various sedges (our smallest sedge moth *Glyphipterix morangella*), and mosses (a purple pyralid or 'deltoid' moth, family Crambidae). Again, there are few species but an abundance of individuals.

Several Chathams trees and shrubs have an abundance of conspicuous fleshy fruits. Matipo (*Myrsine*) in particular is host to sap beetles (Nitidulidae), and caterpillars of a budmoth *Heterocrossa* sp. and the fruit moth *Microcolona* sp. In addition, scale insects infest the fruit clusters.

Some insects dine on different fare on the Chathams. A large red-brown noctuid moth (unnamed) feeds on tarahinau (*Dracophyllum arboreum*), while its mainland relatives all feed on sedges or tussocks. The looper moth *Elvia glaucata*, which on the mainland eats bush lawyer, here eats the introduced blackberry. A group of leafrollers (*Merophyas spp.*) has four endemic species on the Chathams, with one species feeding on wheki and bracken, and three on koromiko – plants that their relatives on the mainland and in Australia do not eat.

The Chatham Island sow thistle weevil (*Stephanorhynchus purus*) does not bore in dead wood as do its New Zealand relatives, but rather in the fleshy petioles and stems of the Chatham Island sow thistle (*Embergeria grandifolia*). It is now known to feed also on ragwort and various thistles, but although clearly no longer dependent on the sow thistle, it is more readily encountered on that host. Because it has broadened its host range to include introduced relatives of sow thistle, this weevil is now relatively common.

The flightless Chatham Island click beetle is most often found on tree trunks at night. It is now rarely encountered on the main islands.

John Marris

Endangered or threatened insects

Endangered or threatened Chatham Islands insects are all large, striking, flightless species, and most are now restricted to weka- and rodent-free islands, including Rangatira and Mangere.

Chatham Island click beetle

Amychus candezei adults are nocturnal, 15–25 millimetres long, and wander on rocks and tree trunks at night. They are most common on the outer islands but can still be seen occasionally on Chatham Island. This beetle has a sister species on small islands in the outer Marlborough Sounds in Cook Strait, and another on the Three Kings Islands.

Chatham Island stag beetle

Geordorcus species are distinctive in shape, being very broad in relation to their length, and the male has impressive arched mandibles (see pages 116 and 118). They are nocturnal. The large C-shaped grubs live in peaty soil, feeding on buried wood and organic matter. The Chatham Island stag beetle (*G. capito*) is found south of the Tuku-a-tamatea River, as well as on Pitt Island and several rodent-free outer islands. Another species, *G. sororum*, which is confined to The Sisters, has recently been described.

Coxella weevil

The distribution of coxella weevils (*Hadramphus spinipennis*) has become reduced over the years, as they are reliant on the presence of their host plant. The striking, knobbly adult browses the leaves, stems and

Coxella weevils are closely associated with their host plant, *Aciphylla dieffenbachii* (coxella). Adult weevils feed on the flowers and foliage at night.

John Marris

particularly flowers of an endemic speargrass, *Aciphylla dieffenbachii* (coxella). The larvae feed underground on its fleshy taproot. However, adult weevils are occasionally found on trunks of hoho (*Pseudopanax chathamicus*), a long way from known speargrass clumps. *Hadramphus* relatives on the mainland are all rare or endangered and feed on speargrasses or punui; one relative on the Poor Knights Islands feeds on the live trunks of karo (*Pittosporum crassifolium*).

Pitt Island longhorn

Xylotoles costatus, 14–20 millimetres long and stoutly ribbed, was first discovered on Pitt Island, but has not been seen there for 100 years. The beetle was rediscovered in 1986 on Rangatira Island. Larvae probably feed in dying karamu trunks. The longhorn may have become extinct on Pitt as a result of predation by mice and weka.

'Thotmus' weevil

This 15-millimetre-long stout weevil (*Thotmus halli*), which seems to be modified for sand dwelling, is possibly extinct. One specimen was collected on Pitt Island about 1907 by Thomas Hall, an itinerant shepherd and beetle collector. Despite much searching, it has not been seen again (see page 162).

The wood-boring Pitt Island longhorn is one of the Chathams' rarest insects. It now appears to survive only on Rangatira Island, where it is associated with karamu.

John Marris

Giant stick insect

The slender, finely spined *Argosarchus horridus* grows up to 15 centimetres. It is not endemic to the Chathams and is rarely encountered, even on Rangatira Island. The eggs can remain viable for more than a year in leaf litter and may not hatch in dry years. Although not threatened, the insect is clearly scarce on the Chathams. Forest restoration may be helpful in the conservation of this stick insect, although on Chatham Island a population has been found in a domestic garden on introduced plants, including blackberry.

Future trends

Before conservation measures for the Chathams invertebrate fauna can be effective, more has to be learned about factors controlling populations. The recovery powers of some insects (and their hosts) can be great; for example, the apparent decline in both coxella and its weevil on Mangere Island in the late 1980s had been reversed by 1992 so that healthy populations of both were found all over the island. Since then the weevil and its host plant have been through another cycle of boom and bust and it appears that the weevil has the ability to destroy local populations of coxella.

Where rodents, weka and pigs are absent, and where the plant cover is little disturbed, the insect communities appear safe enough. It is important that restoration projects on the islands include provision of both appropriate host plants and habitats for insects. For instance, the planned revegetation of Mangere with forest is being designed to preserve the open spaces that are required by coxella and the coxella weevil.

Threats to all island ecosystems on the Chathams come mainly from newly introduced species, brought in as trade with the New Zealand mainland increases, as there are few effective quarantine measures in place. However, many of the significant horticultural and forestry pests present on the mainland are still absent in the Chathams, providing the island economy with a potential advantage. Of all current threats, the greatest are those posed by social wasps, which spread through queens stowing away for the winter in timber, containers and the like, then potentially being transported to the Chathams. Other significant threats come from introduced plant pests and the existing introduced mammals.

Some new arrivals do not persist for lack of suitable habitat, but others go on to become an unwelcome part of the established Chathams fauna. Such faunal change is a normal process over geological time, but the process is being massively accelerated by human trade and transport.

The large New Zealand tunnelweb spider (*Porrhothele antipodiana*) was first recorded from Port Hutt in the 1950s. This specimen was found at Waitangi in 2008. Its impact on Chathams insects is unknown.

Dale Williams

SPIDERS AND HARVESTMEN

Around 40 species of spider from 20 families are currently known from the Chathams, a very small number compared with the estimated New Zealand fauna of 2500–3300 species in 56 families. Sixteen species are unique to the Chathams, although further research may increase this figure. There are no endemic genera.

The endemic sheetweb spider *Cambridgea annulata* feeding on a weta.
John Marris

Many of the species are native to New Zealand and typically have a widespread distribution on the mainland. This suggests they are effective dispersers and probably reached the Chathams by natural means, such as ballooning or rafting. Descent from naturally dispersing colonisers is a plausible explanation for the origin of the endemic spider fauna.

Dispersal aided by humans is another factor, with foreign species such as the whitetailed spider (*Lampona murina*) and the false katipo (*Steatoda capensis*) recently recorded from the Chathams.

The most famous of Chathams spiders is the Rangatira spider (*Dolomedes schauinslandi*), most commonly found on rodent-free Rangatira and Mangere Islands. It has been recorded from Pitt Island, but the introduction of rodents and weka may explain its current absence. With a leg-span of up to 10 centimetres it is a very large spider by New Zealand standards, and capable of taking prey such as weta. Like the related nursery web spider (*Dolomedes minor*) of New Zealand, it constructs a nursery web to protect its young.

The most commonly encountered endemic species is *Cambridgea annulata*, found throughout the Chathams across a wide range of habitats. Occasionally it nearly rivals the Rangatira spider in terms of leg-span, but most specimens are smaller. Other common species include orbweb spiders such as the garden orbweb spider (*Eriophora pustulosa*), and the endemic wolf spider *Anoteropsis ralphi*.

Harvestmen (Opiliones) can also be found in the Chathams – there are several as-yet-unidentified species of Laniatores and the cosmopolitan *Phalangium opilio*, the latter almost certainly introduced by humans.

Phil Sirvid

The large, fearsome-looking Rangatira spider (*Dolomedes schauinslandi*) hunts by night.
John Marris

LAND SNAILS

There is still much to learn about Chatham Islands land snails. Thirty-nine species (including a few undescribed) are known from the Chathams of which 11 (28 per cent) are endemic. This level of endemism is high, and is comparable to the distinct snail faunas of Northland and northwest Nelson. Further species are likely to be discovered.

Diversity is apparently similar to mainland areas. All of the genera are shared with the New Zealand mainland, mirroring the pattern of other faunal and floral groups, where few endemic genera are recognised. About half of the Chathams species are widespread and also occur in northern, central and southern New Zealand. However, some Chathams snails are strikingly different from their mainland relatives, leading to debate over how long they have been isolated, and whether the Chatham Islands could have existed as emergent land for longer than the 2.5 million years claimed by geologists.

The native snails are all small, with shell diameters of 1–10 millimetres. They should not be confused with the much larger introduced garden snail (*Cornu aspersum*), which is unfortunately common on Chatham Island and has recently reached Pitt Island. Native snails live as detritivores mainly in the litter layer, but some are also found in tree forks and under logs, rocks and bark, where they feed on microorganisms associated with plant decay. Fossil shells can be found in shell middens and sand dunes, and have been used to reconstruct ancient environments at archaeological sites. People have modified the vegetation of the Chatham Islands for centuries, including grazing stock over most of Chatham, Pitt, Rangatira and Mangere Islands. This must have had an impact on the land snail fauna, at least with regard to species densities. Two species are known only as fossils. A detailed comparison between fossil and living assemblages of snails could provide further information on the impacts of human settlement on biodiversity.

Karin Mahlfeld

1 mm

Undescribed *Charopa* species, an endemic 4.6mm-diameter land snail recorded from Rangatira Island.

David Roscoe

CHAPTER NINE

BIRDS AND LIZARD

Birds form a large part of the Chatham Islands' identity and international profile. Moriori referred to themselves as manu (birds), and many of their tree carvings (rakau momori) show stylised human-bird forms. Their protein was largely sourced from birds and the sea, with bones of over 50 bird species found in their camp middens. Prominent among them are bones of taiko (Magenta petrel) and other petrels, albatrosses, parea (Chatham Island pigeon), rails, tui, parakeets, swans and ducks.

The seasonal harvest of albatross chicks (hopo) from outlying islets required skill, courage and careful attention to traditional protocols. The only sea-going craft were wash-through rafts (waka korari), constructed from bundles of dried flower stalks of harakeke (flax). Following the arrival of Maori and the subjugation of Moriori in 1835, Ngati Mutunga continued to harvest hopo, using sturdier European whale boats.

Harvest of birds and their eggs continues, with hunting of weka, swans and ducks, and harvest of swan eggs. Though it is currently prohibited, there is also interest in resumption of harvest of hopo and titi (the chicks of sooty shearwater, or muttonbirds).

Albatrosses remain of great importance to both Moriori and Ngati Mutunga. The Moriori Kopinga Marae, opened in 2005, is designed in the form of an albatross. The ceremonial wearing of tufts of albatross feathers (raukura) by both imi/iwi shows respect for the prophets Nunuku Whenua (Moriori) and Te Whiti Rongomai (Ngati Mutunga).

Northern royal albatross and chick, Forty Fours.

Tui De Roy

Top: Chatham Island tui feeding on flowering Chatham Island flax (harakeke). Don Merton

Buff weka.

Darren Scott

The 'bird identity' of Chatham Islanders persists, with those born in mainland New Zealand referred to as 'Kiwi', and those born on the Chatham Islands referred to as 'Weka'. This last name is somewhat ironic, for although hunting and eating weka is an important part of Chatham Islands' culture, the birds were introduced to the islands from mainland New Zealand only in 1905.

The dramatic rescue of the black robin from imminent extinction during 1976–89 and the rediscovery of the Chatham Island taiko in 1978 made the Chatham Islands famous among birdwatchers and conservationists. These two species have assumed icon status, and have been featured proudly on souvenir clothing, postage stamps, local currency and even beer branding.

The ongoing – and to date successful – taiko and black robin recovery programmes are a justifiable source of pride. However, there are many other Chatham Islands bird species that have responded well to applied research and careful management. Some of their stories are told later in the chapter. To appreciate why so many Chatham Islands bird species have become extinct, or have required intensive management to avert extinction, it is necessary to understand what caused their decline.

Human impacts

When Moriori reached the Chatham Islands about 500 years ago there were at least 64 species of breeding birds present, 33 of which were forms found only on the Chathams. Although 52 per cent of Chatham birds were recognisably distinct from their mainland relatives, most of this endemism was at the species and subspecies level, reflecting the recent (2.5 million years ago) re-emergence of the Chatham Island

Black robins were confined to Mangere and Rangatira Islands in 2008.

Elwyn Wilson

landmass and its availability for colonisation. Only three of the birds are recognisably distinct at the genus level: the large Hawkins' rail (*Diaphorapteryx hawkinsi*), the tiny Chatham Island rail (*Cabalus modestus*), and a large flightless duck (*Pachyanas chathamica*). Regrettably all three are extinct.

Hunting and the introduction of the Pacific rat (kiore) caused extinction of 15 bird species (nine endemic) before the first European naturalists arrived in 1840. Notable among the lost species were six waterfowl (black swan, a shelduck, New Zealand merganser, Scarlett's duck, New Zealand scaup, and the Chatham Island flightless duck), a crested penguin, Hawkins' rail, a coot, a raven, a kaka parrot, and Forbes' snipe, which was larger than the surviving Chatham Island snipe. Four of the extinct species (the penguin, shelduck, kaka and a gadfly petrel) have yet to be formally described and named.

The rate of loss increased further with European settlement, due to introduction of further predators (especially cats, Norway rats, ship rats, mice, pigs, possums and weka) and clearance of much of the forest for farming. At least seven species became extinct after 1840, four of which were endemic (Chatham Island rail, Dieffenbach's rail, Chatham Island bellbird and Chatham Island fernbird). During the same period seven bird species were deliberately introduced to the Chathams (including reintroduction of the black swan), and a further nine species introduced to mainland New Zealand found their own way to the Chathams and established breeding populations.

Most of these introduced species and other recent colonists (for example welcome swallow, spur-winged plover and white-faced heron) occupy farmland and so are unlikely to compete with native Chatham Islands species. However, mallards are hybridising with and displacing the native grey duck, and European starlings compete for nest holes with the black robin and both parakeet species. Introduced birds are also believed to be the source of avian pox that affects black robins and other endemic forest birds.

The net result of species losses, introductions and self-introductions is that there are now 68 breeding bird species on the Chatham Islands, only 18 (26 per cent) of which are endemic. This situation would be even worse if introduced predators had reached the smaller outlying islands. Twenty-two Chatham Islands bird species (including six endemic forms) survive or breed only on islands lacking mammalian predators.

Land birds

There are very few native land birds left on main Chatham Island. The six widespread species are the Chatham Island fantail and pipit, the Australasian harrier, and the self-introduced silvereye, welcome swallow and spur-winged plover. Fantails occur in gardens and all forest

Known only from subfossil bones, the Chatham Island flightless duck is placed in its own genus (*Pachyanas*); its relationships are uncertain.

Painting by Paul Martinson, Museum of New Zealand, Te Papa Tongarewa, MA_I043775

The extinct Chatham Island fernbird is known from 43 specimens collected on Mangere Island between 1868 and 1892.

Painting by Paul Martinson, Museum of New Zealand, Te Papa Tongarewa, MA_I043740

Chatham Island red-crowned parakeets occur on the four largest islands, but their stronghold is on Rangatira Island.

Don Merton

Below left: Male Chatham Island warbler. Very abundant on Rangatira and Mangere Islands, this endemic warbler is also present on Pitt Island and southern Chatham Island.

Don Merton

Below right: Chatham Island tui feeding on flowering harakeke (flax), Rangatira Island. Tui are rarely seen on Chatham Island, but are common on Pitt Island.

Don Merton

remnants, while pipits are common around the coast, on roadsides, and on close-cropped pasture.

Three endemic taxa survive in the forests of the southern tablelands: parea, Chatham Island red-crowned parakeet and Chatham Island warbler. Parakeets and warblers can be seen in Thomas Mohi Tuuta (Rangaika) Scenic Reserve, and all three occur in the Tuku Nature Reserve and nearby covenants. Parea can often be seen from the public road at Awatotara, and occasionally visit reserves further north.

Native forest birds are more readily seen on Pitt Island, where the Chatham Island tui and tomtit thrive in the absence of rats and possums. They are readily seen in Ellen Elizabeth Preece Conservation Covenant, along with Chatham Island red-crowned parakeets, warblers and fantails. This privately owned forest remnant is surrounded by a cat-proof fence, and is the site where attempts have been made to restore black robins, Chatham petrels and Chatham Island snipe to Pitt Island.

The strongholds for most of the endemic forest birds (other than parea) are the outlying nature reserves of Rangatira (South East) Island and Mangere Island. Mangere Island and neighbouring Little Mangere Island (Tapuaenuku) are the only sites where Forbes' parakeet survives.

With the exception of the harrier, pipit, swallow and spur-winged plover, the common birds of farmland on Chatham and Pitt Islands are introduced species, including buff weka, starling, skylark, redpoll, goldfinch, dunnock (hedge sparrow), blackbird and song thrush. Southern black-backed gulls and brown skuas also occur on farmland, the latter mainly on Pitt Island, south of the Owenga Road, and near Waitangi West.

Male Chatham Island tomtit, Rangatira Island. Tomtits were last seen on Chatham Island about 1976, but they persist in forest on Pitt Island.
Don Merton

Chatham Island shag.
Don Hadden

Waterfowl and rails

The Chatham Islands formerly held a diverse assemblage of ducks and a swan. Eight species became extinct, leaving the grey duck as the sole representative. Black swans were reintroduced in the 1890s, and mallards (introduced to mainland New Zealand) have self-colonised. With the exception of the vast flocks of swans on Te Whanga Lagoon, most Chatham Islands wetlands now have few waterfowl present.

The rails of the Chatham Islands were similarly affected by human hunting and predation by introduced mammals. Four species became extinct, and two further species (marsh crake and spotless crake) are rarely reported on the Chatham Islands, with the latter possibly extinct there. Only the pukeko and the introduced weka remain common.

Coastal birds

Wild coastlines are a feature of the Chatham Islands. While the long sandy beaches generally have few birds other than southern black-backed gulls, rocky coasts and headlands have more diversity, including nesting and roosting colonies of Chatham Island shags and Pitt Island shags. Contrary to their names, both these shag species occur on both sides of Pitt Strait. The third shag (cormorant) species is the black shag, which occurs on freshwater wetlands, the brackish Te Whanga Lagoon and around the coast. It nests among harakeke (flax) swamps on Chatham Island.

Chatham Island oystercatchers occur around the coasts of the four largest islands, but are most readily seen on the northwest coast of Chatham Island and the east coast of Pitt Island. Shore plover can be seen from boats close offshore from Rangatira and Mangere Islands, and they occasionally visit the east coast of Pitt Island. The similarly

Pitt Island shag.
Rod Morris, DOC

sized banded dotterel is patchily distributed on coastal pasture, open dunelands and saltmarsh on both main islands.

Migratory waders (especially bar-tailed godwit and lesser knot) are most often present on the northern and eastern shores of Te Whanga Lagoon, while turnstones can be found on rocky headlands around the northern coasts in summer. Pied stilts are frequently seen (and breed) around Te Whanga Lagoon and nearby lakes.

Brown skua feeding on a dead blue penguin, Rangatira Island. Note the attendant blowflies (Calliphoridae).

Don Merton

The Chatham Island blue penguin breeds around the shoreline of all but the steepest islands. As they visit their nests at night, the main signs of their presence are footprints on sandy beaches, and droppings outside their nesting burrows and crevices.

Other birds of Chatham Islands coasts include white-fronted terns, red-billed gulls, brown skuas (especially on Pitt Island), spur-winged plovers and white-faced herons. Weka also forage along the coast, especially in rocky bays, and Arctic skuas often chase white-fronted terns close offshore in summer, forcing them to drop or disgorge fish.

Birds of the open ocean

The Chatham Islands are internationally important breeding grounds for ocean-going seabirds, with seven taxa having their main or only world breeding sites on the islands. Endemic forms include Chatham Island mollymawk (albatross) on The Pyramid, Chatham Island taiko on southwest Chatham Island, Chatham petrel on Rangatira Island, and the Chatham Island fulmar prion on The Pyramid and the Forty

Chatham Island mollymawk on The Pyramid, which is the sole breeding site for this distinctive albatross.

Tui De Roy

Fours. The Forty Fours and The Sisters are important breeding sites for northern royal albatrosses, Pacific mollymawks and northern giant petrels. Rangatira Island has huge colonies of broad-billed prions and white-faced storm petrels, plus sooty shearwaters, common diving petrels and grey-backed storm petrels. All these species occur in lesser numbers on Mangere Island, which is a major breeding site for fairy prions.

Landings on the main seabird-breeding islands are by permit only, or require permission from island owners. However, many species can be seen from boats around the islands, and northern giant petrels, sooty shearwaters and Pacific mollymawks are readily seen from headlands.

An estimated 330,000 pairs of broad-billed prions breed on Rangatira Island.

Helen Gummer

Research and recovery programmes

Most Chatham Islands bird species have been protected through the establishment of reserves and covenants, or simply because their breeding islands are difficult to land on. However, several species have been the focus of intensive recovery programmes in addition to protection of their breeding habitat. Eight brief case studies are presented here.

Black robin

The most famous bird of the Chatham Islands, the black robin, came as close to extinction as it is possible to get and yet recover – one fertile female. The sole remaining population was confined to a tiny forest remnant on the top of Little Mangere Island for over 80 years. A combination of human impacts (clearing a helipad) and natural processes (storm events, undermining of trees by numerous sooty shearwater

Black robin fledglings being fed by their Chatham Island tomtit foster-mother during the most intensive phase of the black robin recovery programme. Rangatira Island, 1985.

Don Merton

The Chatham Island taiko is one of the world's rarest birds. The 2007–08 breeding season was the best on record, with the 15 known breeding pairs raising 13 chicks that were all translocated to Sweetwater Conservation Covenant before fledging.

Graeme Taylor

Parea (Chatham Island pigeons) have increased greatly in response to sustained feral cat and possum control in the Tuku Nature Reserve and adjacent covenants.

Dan Palmer

burrows, and rampant growth of *Muehlenbeckia* vine) caused rapid deterioration of the forest in the 1970s, and all seven remaining black robins were moved to Mangere Island in 1976–77. The population reached a low of just five birds in 1980 before a careful programme of cross-fostering (mainly using the closely related Chatham Island tomtit on Rangatira Island) led to an increase to about 80 birds in 1989. Cross-fostering ceased in 1989, and monitoring of every bird and every nest was stopped in 1998, at which stage there were about 200 birds (50 on Mangere and 150 on Rangatira).

Forty black robins were moved to Ellen Elizabeth Preece Conservation Covenant (Pitt Island) between 2001 and 2005. Unfortunately none was seen there after November 2007. It is believed that the abundant mouse population in the covenant removed much of the robins' spider and insect food. The population on Rangatira and Mangere Islands declined to about 150 birds in 2007, but it is not yet known whether this was solely due to removal of birds for translocation, or whether other factors were responsible.

Chatham Island taiko (Magenta petrel)

For 111 years the scientific world knew of the Magenta petrel from a single specimen collected in the central South Pacific in 1867. From 1972 ornithologist David Crockett started to investigate the possibility that the Magenta petrel was the same as the taiko, a burrow-nesting seabird that was harvested in large numbers for food from southern Chatham Island up to the early 1900s. This theory was confirmed by the capture of two Chatham Island taiko near the Tuku-a-tamatea River on 1 January 1978. The first nest burrows were found in 1987–88, and by 2008 about 15 breeding burrows were known in and near the Tuku Nature Reserve. The slow increase in known burrows is due to a combination of predator control (mainly targeting feral cats and rats), and ongoing burrow searches using radio-tracking and trained dogs. All 21 chicks produced in 2007 and 2008 were moved to the predator-fenced Sweetwater Conservation Covenant in order to start a new colony less reliant on predator control.

Parea

The stronghold of the parea is the forested areas of southwest main Chatham. Fortunately this area includes the breeding grounds of the taiko, and parea have benefited from associated land protection and feral cat and possum control. The population reached a low of about 40 birds in 1990, but is now estimated at over 200. Birds are regularly seen as far north as Te Matarae, and occasionally range to Thomas Mohi Tuuta (Rangaika) Scenic Reserve, Henga Scenic Reserve, Nikau Bush Conservation Area and Wharekauri Station.

Chatham Island oystercatcher

Oystercatchers were affected by the combined impacts of changed land use and the introduction of predators, especially feral cats. On sandy beaches oystercatchers nest between the high-tide line and vegetation at the front of the foredunes. Originally the foredunes had gentle profiles and were sparsely vegetated with pingao, sand sedge (*Carex pumila*) and Chatham Island forget-me-not, providing suitable nesting habitat. Following the 1890s introduction of marram grass to stabilise dunes, the foredunes became densely vegetated, and formed a steep profile rising cliff-like from the stormline. Oystercatchers then had only a very narrow strip of beach to nest on at the foot of the dune, where the nests were vulnerable to storm waves, predators hunting along the high-tide line, and crushing by off-road vehicles. As a consequence the population declined to only 142 birds by 1998. Management has included predator control (cats and weka), spraying of marram followed by planting native species, and gradually moving oystercatcher nests up the beach away from the high-tide line. These measures led to a minimum estimate of 320 birds in 2005.

Chatham petrel

Bone deposits reveal that the Chatham petrel nested on Chatham and Pitt Islands, but by the time scientists discovered the species in 1893 it was confined to Rangatira and was very rare. During the 1990s studies of the few known nests revealed that most chicks were being killed by the vastly more numerous broad-billed prions when the latter were prospecting for nesting burrows. Management of this conflict initially required checking each Chatham petrel burrow three times a night,

Chatham Island oystercatcher.
Don Hadden

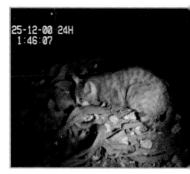

Feral cat eating Chatham Island oystercatcher eggs at night, captured on infrared video.
Peter Moore

The Chatham petrel population on Rangatira Island was declining towards extinction due to burrow competition from broad-billed prions. The petrels are now recovering following innovative management, and chicks have been translocated to predator-fenced sites on Pitt Island and Chatham Island.

Don Merton

and culling any prions found inside. Carefully designed trials led to the development of neoprene (wetsuit material) screens placed over the tunnel entrances of artificial burrows (see page 155). An inverted T-shaped slit in the screen allowed breeding Chatham petrels to enter to reach their egg or chick, but prospecting prions were discouraged by the screen, which concealed the burrow entrance. In this way up to 130 Chatham petrel burrows were protected each year, and up to 115 chicks successfully reared by their parents. This larger crop of young allowed some to be 'harvested' for translocation elsewhere. During 2002–05, 200 chicks were moved to the predator-fenced Ellen Elizabeth Preece Conservation Covenant on Pitt Island and hand-fed pureed sardines until they fledged. Birds started to return to the release site two or three years later; the first locally reared chick fledged in 2006, with four in 2007 and seven in 2008. Translocation of Chatham petrels to main Chatham Island began with the transfer of 47 chicks to the predator-fenced Sweetwater Conservation Covenant in April 2008.

Forbes' parakeet

The original distribution of Forbes' parakeet is poorly known, as its bones are currently indistinguishable from the similarly sized Chatham Island red-crowned parakeet. Like the black robin, Forbes' parakeets became confined to 19-hectare Little Mangere Island, but recolonised the adjacent 131-hectare Mangere Island following the removal of sheep in 1968. There are historical specimens of Forbes' parakeets from Pitt Island, and since 1982 vagrant birds have been seen associating with red-crowned parakeets on Pitt, Chatham and Rangatira Islands.

For many years considered a subspecies of the New Zealand yellow-

Forbes' parakeet feeding on *Carex trifida* seeds, Little Mangere Island. Forbes' parakeets are confined to Mangere and Little Mangere Islands, with vagrant birds occasionally seen on other islands.

Mike Bell

crowned parakeet, the Forbes' parakeet has been shown by genetic research to be distinct at species level. Further genetic research investigated the introgression of red-crowned parakeet genes into the Forbes' parakeet gene pool. Hybridisation occurred sporadically over the 10,000 or so years since red-crowned parakeets colonised the Chatham Islands and became sympatric with the Forbes' parakeets already there. It became prevalent as both species recolonised Mangere Island in the 1970s and 1980s, and was managed by culling of hybrids and red-crowned parakeets through to 1999. Since then the level of hybridisation has stabilised, with hybrids making up less than 10 per cent of the total parakeet population on Mangere Island, which is below the threshold for management intervention. From a population low of fewer than 30 birds in 1970, there are now estimated to be over 750 Forbes' parakeets on Mangere Island.

Shore plover

Shore plover once occurred around mainland New Zealand, but predation by introduced mammals resulted in their elimination from their entire range apart from 249-hectare Rangatira Island (about

Rangatira Island is the stronghold for shore plover, which has also been reintroduced to Mangere Island.

Helen Gummer

130 birds), and 9-hectare Western Reef (about 20 birds), both in the Chatham Islands. The latter population was only discovered in 1999, but had declined to a single male by 2003. The most likely cause for their decline was contamination of intertidal feeding areas by the increasing fur seal population on Western Reef. The last Western Reef bird was captured in June 2003 and taken to the National Wildlife Centre at Mt Bruce in the Wairarapa, where his offspring now make up about half the captive shore plover population.

The recovery programme for shore plover has focused on protecting the main population on Rangatira, restoring a population on Mangere Island by translocating juvenile birds from Rangatira, and using captive-reared birds to restore shore plover to islands around the New Zealand mainland that are free of mammalian predators.

Chatham Island snipe

The Chatham Island snipe came perilously close to extinction in the 1950s. Formerly present throughout the Chatham Islands, by 1900 snipe were extirpated by predators everywhere except on Rangatira Island. The island had been farmed since 1842, and very little of the dense ground cover favoured by snipe remained. The removal of stock in 1959 and 1961 restored dense cover, and there are now over 1200 snipe on the island. The New Zealand Wildlife Service reintroduced 23 snipe to Mangere Island in 1970, where they thrived. An attempt to reintroduce snipe to Pitt Island began in April 2008, when 20 were released within the predator-fenced Ellen Elizabeth Preece Conservation Covenant (see page 153). Snipe have also been reported from Star Keys, Little Mangere and Rabbit Islands.

Chatham Island snipe are abundant on Rangatira Island, and have been reintroduced to Mangere and Pitt Islands.

Don Merton

DOC staff pass boxes containing Chatham petrel chicks over the predator-proof fence that surrounds the Ellen Elizabeth Preece Conservation Covenant (Caravan Bush) on Pitt Island.

Helen Gummer

The future

A major focus of bird conservation programmes on the Chatham Islands is making the islands' unique birds more accessible to residents and their guests. This is expected to continue through predator control and/or predator-proof fencing at selected sites on the two main islands, and translocations of locally extinct birds. Attempted translocations have included the Chatham petrel, Chatham Island taiko, shore plover, Chatham Island snipe, parea, Chatham Island tomtit and black robin. Future candidates for translocations include the Chatham Island tui, Forbes' parakeet, and several species no longer present on the Chatham Islands (such as brown teal, fernbird and bellbird).

Further introductions of threatened birds to Chatham Island are limited by the high cost of building and maintaining predator-proof fences. The first predator-exclosure on the main island (Sweetwater Conservation Covenant) was built on private land using funds raised by the Chatham Island Taiko Trust. The collaboration between landowners, private conservation organisations and government (local or central) exemplified by the Sweetwater fence and associated pest control and seabird restoration is a pointer for the future. If a rodent- and cat-proof fence could be constructed around one of the northern forest remnants, there is the potential for the full range of surviving Chatham land birds to be restored to the main island.

Another area of huge potential is restoration of waterfowl communities through a combination of habitat management, predator and competitor control, and release of captive-reared birds. The surviving grey duck population will need active management to prevent it being displaced and genetically swamped by the introduced mallard. Other species (potentially including brown teal, shoveler, scaup and shelduck) will require reintroduction from the New Zealand mainland, provided sufficient precautions are taken to prevent introduction of diseases not present in Chathams bird populations.

People have had a huge negative impact on Chatham Islands birds. However, they have also shown enormous capacity for positive impacts through innovation and sheer hard work. Much has been achieved in securing Chatham Islands birds from extinction since 1950. Provided locals and the wider New Zealand community continue to value their natural heritage, Chatham Islands birds should continue to provide beacons of hope and inspiration for conservationists worldwide.

Common name	Scientific name	Threat status
Chatham Island mollymawk	*Thalassarche eremita*	Naturally uncommon
Chatham Island fulmar prion	*Pachyptila crassirostris pyramidalis*	Naturally uncommon
Chatham petrel	*Pterodroma axillaris*	Nationally vulnerable
Chatham Island taiko	*P. magentae*	Nationally critical
† Gadfly petrel sp.	*Pterodroma* undescribed sp.	Extinct (subfossil)
Chatham Island blue penguin	*Eudyptula minor chathamensis*	Naturally uncommon
† Chatham Island crested penguin	*Eudyptes* undescribed sp.	Extinct (subfossil)
Chatham Island shag	*Leucocarbo onslowi*	Nationally endangered
Pitt Island shag	*Stictocarbo featherstoni*	Nationally endangered
† Chatham Island shelduck	*Tadorna* undescribed sp.	Extinct (subfossil)
† Chatham Island flightless duck	*Pachyanas chathamica*	Extinct (subfossil)
† Dieffenbach's rail	*Gallirallus dieffenbachii*	Extinct (recent)
† Chatham Island rail	*Cabalus modestus*	Extinct (recent)
† Hawkins' rail	*Diaphorapteryx hawkinsi*	Extinct (recent)
† Chatham Island coot	*Fulica chathamensis*	Extinct (subfossil)
Chatham Island oystercatcher	*Haematopus chathamensis*	Nationally critical
Chatham Island snipe	*Coenocorypha pusilla*	Nationally vulnerable
† Forbes' snipe	*C. chathamica*	Extinct (subfossil)
Parea (Chatham Island pigeon)	*Hemiphaga chathamensis*	Nationally critical
† Chatham Island kaka	*Nestor* undescribed sp.	Extinct (subfossil)
Chatham Island red-crowned parakeet	*Cyanoramphus novaezelandiae chathamensis*	Naturally uncommon
Forbes' parakeet	*C. forbesi*	Nationally endangered
Chatham Island pipit	*Anthus novaeseelandiae chathamensis*	Naturally uncommon
† Chatham Island fernbird	*Bowdleria rufescens*	Extinct (recent)
Chatham Island warbler	*Gerygone albofrontata*	Nationally vulnerable
Chatham Island fantail	*Rhipidura fuliginosa penita*	Naturally uncommon
Chatham Island tomtit	*Petroica macrocephala chathamensis*	Nationally endangered
Black robin	*P. traversi*	Nationally critical
† Chatham Island bellbird	*Anthornis melanocephala*	Extinct (recent)
Chatham Island tui	*Prosthemadera novaeseelandiae chathamensis*	Nationally endangered
† Chatham Island raven	*Corvus moriorum*	Extinct (subfossil)

CHATHAM ISLAND SKINK

The Chatham Island skink (*Oligosoma nigriplantare nigriplantare*) was discovered on Pitt Island by Henry Travers in 1871. He remarked that it was not known from the main island, but was abundant on the small mammal-free islands south of Pitt Strait. This remains the case, plus they are common on The Sisters and Forty Fours. On Pitt Island the skink is common only within the cat-proof fence of the Ellen Elizabeth Preece Conservation Covenant.

The absence of skinks on Chatham Island was probably due to the introduction of Pacific rats (kiore) by Moriori. The main island and islets within 100 metres of its shores are still the only islands in the group that have rats, although three species are now present (Norway rat, ship rat and Pacific rat).

The Chatham Island skink is highly variable in size and colour. It is considered the same species as the common skink of central New Zealand, but is subspecifically distinct. No other lizard species are known from the Chatham Islands.

Chatham Island skinks, Rangatira Island. Helen Gummer

Table opposite: Endemic birds of the Chatham Islands. Three further species almost qualify as endemic: northern royal albatross (nationally vulnerable) and Pacific mollymawk (naturally uncommon) have over 99 per cent of their breeding populations on the Chatham Islands, but also have small breeding populations on Otago Peninsula and the Three Kings Islands respectively; shore plover (nationally critical) originally occurred around mainland New Zealand, but became confined to the Chatham Islands before being reintroduced to a few small islands off the mainland coast. Species marked with † have become extinct since human contact (as have a further eight non-endemic species, three of which are now globally extinct – New Zealand little bittern, New Zealand merganser and Scarlett's duck).

CHAPTER TEN

MANAGING THE RESOURCE

The Chatham Islands are of international conservation importance, owing to the high number of bird, insect and plant species that occur nowhere else, and the islands' unique human history. Many of the endemic species have become extinct or severely threatened because of habitat loss and other human impacts, especially the introduction of browsing and predatory mammals. Efforts to conserve the Chatham Islands' biodiversity and archaeological heritage began in the 1950s and continue apace. This chapter summarises the work undertaken and some of the key sites protected.

The workforce

The Department of Conservation (DOC) is the main agency responsible for conservation management on the Chatham Islands. Formed in 1987 through an amalgamation of parts of various previous government departments, DOC is charged with promoting the conservation of New Zealand's natural and historic resources. This includes managing lands held under the Conservation Act and Reserves Act, advocating for conservation of natural and historic resources generally, and (where not inconsistent with conservation) fostering the use of these resources for recreation.

Until 1987 conservation roles on the Chatham Islands were split between the Department of Lands and Survey, administering land protected under the Reserves Act, and the New Zealand Wildlife Service,

---

Top: Landing sign and hut, Mangere Island Nature Reserve. Helen Gummer

caring for threatened birds protected under the Wildlife Act. New Zealand-based Wildlife Service officers and scientists visited annually from 1972, with the major focus being intensive research and management of the black robin. Conservation did not have a permanent staff presence on the Chatham Islands until 1983, when Malcolm Campbell was appointed as the Lands and Survey ranger. The resident workforce had increased to three by early 1987, with Rob Chappell assisted by local men Richard Peirce and George Tuuta. All three transferred to the newly formed Department of Conservation, with Chappell appointed as the first Chatham Islands field centre manager, reporting to DOC's Canterbury Conservancy. Much of the fieldwork was still undertaken by non-resident staff, but this has changed over time as the local conservation workforce has grown.

Dave Lumley (with eight permanent staff) was the field centre manager in late 1997 when a departmental restructuring led to the creation of the Chatham Islands Area Office, and transfer of administration to Wellington Conservancy. A decade later Ken Hunt (as area manager) was managing a team of 16 permanent staff and up to eight seasonal staff.

DOC staff attending the March 2000 wildfire that threatened the Tuku Nature Reserve.
DOC

The workplace

Rangatira (South East) Island became the first reserve on the Chatham Islands when it was purchased from its Maori owners in 1953. This was followed by the purchase of Mangere Island in 1966, and of southern Pitt Island in 1973, much of which was reserved. Largely owing to community opposition to the potential loss of productive land, the government has not actively pursued land purchase for reservation subsequently. However, the network of reserves in public ownership

Rangatira (South East) Island Nature Reserve protects the largest Chathams populations of 15 bird species, eight of them endemic. Pitt Island and the Mangere Islands lie beyond.

Hamish Campbell

has continued to grow incrementally through gifting of land, land transfers during leasehold and freeholding negotiations, and occasional purchases. DOC currently manages about 6520 hectares of public land on the Chatham Islands as reserves – about 8.1 per cent of the total land area. A further 2935 hectares of private land (3.8 per cent) is under some form of covenanted protection or land management agreement.

Public land that is managed as reserves on the Chatham Islands is held either under the Reserves Act (nature, historic and scenic reserves) or under the Conservation Act (conservation areas).

Nature reserves

Apart from national reserves, nature reserves offer the highest level of protection available under the Reserves Act. They protect and preserve indigenous flora or fauna or natural features that are of such rarity, scientific interest or importance, so that their protection and preservation are in the public interest. Access to nature reserves is by permit only and is generally allowed only for approved management or research activities. There are three nature reserves on the Chatham Islands.

Rangatira (South East Island) Nature Reserve: Following his visit in 1937, prominent New Zealand scientist Sir Charles Fleming was instrumental in lobbying for the purchase of 249-hectare Rangatira as a sanctuary. This occurred in 1953, and the island was gazetted as a flora and fauna reserve the following year. Since the last few sheep were removed in 1961, the vegetation has recovered spectacularly.

Rangatira is one of the world's premier bird islands. Free from introduced mammals, it holds the major populations of New Zealand shore plover, Chatham petrel, black robin, Chatham Island snipe, tomtit, tui and red-crowned parakeet. It may be the only site where the Pitt Island longhorn beetle persists, and is an important site for many other large flightless invertebrates that are vulnerable to rodent predation. Vast numbers of burrowing seabirds nest on the island, including hundreds of thousands of broad-billed prions and white-faced storm petrels.

Because of the density of seabird burrows, the island habitat is extremely fragile. Since the removal of stock, several threatened plant species have recovered or established, including keketerehe, coxella, and Chatham Island forget-me-not, sow thistle and button-daisy.

Mangere Island Nature Reserve: Mangere Island (131 hectares) was purchased by the government, with funding help from the Royal Forest and Bird Protection Society of New Zealand, in 1966. The last of the sheep were removed two years later. Very little forest was left on the island, so to begin the process of revegetation the Wildlife Service planted Chatham Island akeake and harakeke from 1974 to 1979, again

Seabird burrows under forest on Rangatira (South East Island) Nature Reserve.

Graham Wood

with the assistance of Forest and Bird. An annual replanting programme using mainly Chatham Island akeake, grown on Chatham Island, resumed in 1991. Between 1995 and 2008 the rearing and planting of up to 6000 akeake per year was done under contract by Bruce and Liz Tuanui, while DOC staff planted lesser numbers of other forest species to diversify the older plantings.

Cats were introduced to Mangere Island in about 1891 to control rabbits, and were successful in eradicating them – together with many endemic bird species, including black robin, Forbes' parakeet, Chatham Island snipe and the now-extinct Chatham Island bellbird, fernbird and rail. Cats were shot by visiting shearing gangs and are believed to have been eradicated during the 1950s.

In 1976–77 the entire world population of black robins (seven birds) was shifted from neighbouring Little Mangere Island to a 10-hectare forest remnant on the eastern end of Mangere Island. For six years this was the species' sole home, until five birds were moved to Rangatira in 1983. During this period Forbes' parakeets naturally recolonised Mangere Island from Little Mangere Island.

Mangere Island also has a large seabird population, which is continuing to increase as woody plants gradually overcome the thick grass sward and help to make the soil accessible for burrowing. Mangere Island and Little Mangere Island hold the only population of Forbes' parakeet, and Mangere Island has the largest populations of coxella and coxella weevil. Chatham Island snipe were successfully reintroduced to Mangere Island in 1970, and New Zealand shore plover in 2001.

Tuku Nature Reserve: This 1239-hectare reserve in the southwest of Chatham Island was gifted to the people of New Zealand by Manuel and Evelyn Tuanui in 1983, primarily to protect the critically endangered Chatham Island taiko. It is part of the largest forest left in the Chathams, and contains a number of other threatened animals and plants, notably parea, Chatham Island red-crowned parakeet and Barker's koromiko.

Tuku Nature Reserve holds the main populations of Chatham Island taiko and parea (Chatham Island pigeon).

Colin Miskelly

Along with the adjacent 1200-hectare South Chatham Conservation Covenant, the reserve is fenced to prevent domestic stock from damaging vegetation, and the forest is recovering well. DOC commits considerable resources to the Tuku Nature Reserve and South Chatham Conservation Covenant, controlling predators (cats, rats and weka) of the taiko and parea, as well as browsing animals (possums, sheep, cattle and pigs).

Historic reserves

Historic reserves protect and preserve places, objects and natural features that are of historic, archaeological, cultural and educational interest. Archaeological sites have the added protection of the Historic Places Act. There are three historic reserves on the Chatham Islands, all near the northeast corner of Chatham Island. One of these has the additional protection and recognition of being designated a national historic reserve. The only other site in New Zealand to receive this recognition is the Cook Landing Site National Historic Reserve at Gisborne.

Forest regeneration in J. M. Barker (Hapupu) National Historic Reserve, 15 years after fencing.

Don Hadden

J. M. Barker (Hapupu) National Historic Reserve: For the Moriori imi of Rekohu, Hapupu has special cultural and spiritual significance. Rakau momori (dendroglyphs or tree carvings) here are among the few remaining visible signs of pre-European Moriori culture. The carvings depict Moriori karapuna (ancestors) and symbols of the natural world, such as patiki (flounder) and birds. The images were carved on living kopi trees; as the trees age and die, the rakau momori decrease in number.

Gifted by Barker Bros Ltd in 1979, this 30-hectare reserve was fenced in 1980. Forest regeneration has been spectacular, with Chatham Island mahoe, akeake, matipo and kopi filling the canopy and understorey. The reserve may be visited at any time; a short walking track leads past several rakau momori.

Taia Bush Historic Reserve: Taia Bush (34 hectares) is located 8 kilometres south of Hapupu. As with Hapupu, Taia Bush was set aside because of rakau momori carved in large kopi trees. Taia Bush was gifted by Sunday and Elsie Hough in 1981.

Taia Farm Historic Reserve: Purchased by the government in 2002, Taia Farm (1199 hectares) covers most of the land south of Hapupu to the Te Whanga Lagoon outlet, excluding the three lakes (Makuku, Kairae and Taia) and their margins, and Taia Bush Historic Reserve. Several of the forest remnants contain rakau momori carved in kopi trees. Taia Farm Historic Reserve is to be vested with the Hokotehi Moriori Trust.

Taia Farm Historic Reserve occupies the strip of low-lying land between Te Whanga Lagoon and Hanson Bay, surrounding several dune lakes.

Peter Johnson

Scenic reserves

Scenic reserves protect and preserve areas that are of scenic interest or that possess such beauty or natural features that their protection and preservation are desirable in the public interest, both for their intrinsic worth and for the benefit, enjoyment and use of the public. There are six scenic reserves on Chatham Island and three on Pitt Island. Members of the public are welcome to enter scenic reserves at any time, but all plants, animals and historical and archaeological features are protected from removal or disturbance. Some sites require access via private land, and permission to do so must be sought and granted first.

Chatham Island scenic reserves

Thomas Mohi Tuuta (Rangaika) Scenic Reserve: This 407-hectare reserve was part of land leased in perpetuity by Thomas and Annie Tuuta but later handed back to the Crown. It contains good examples of peatland plant communities of the southern tablelands (see Chapter 5). The reserve was fenced by the Department of Lands and Survey in 1981; the forest is regenerating well, and has outstanding ground and filmy fern populations. Tableland plants occurring within the reserve include Barker's koromiko, keketerehe, Cox's matipo, Moriori flax, and Chatham Island aster, speargrass and bamboo-rush.

A full day is required to walk through the reserve from the Owenga Road. A track marked with poles starts at the road sign and follows a firebreak across private land to the reserve, about 3.5 kilometres from the road. Visitors should be physically fit and well equipped for weather changes.

Henga Scenic Reserve is the most accessible forest reserve for visitors, located close to the junction of North Road and Airport Road, with the entrance by Chatham Lodge.

Peter Johnson

Henga Scenic Reserve: Henga was gifted to the Crown in 1981 by John and Denise Sutherland, and fenced in 1982. The 170-hectare reserve contains excellent examples of coastal forest and sand-dune vegetation, including threatened plants, e.g. Chatham Island forget-me-not and sow thistle. Access is from Chatham Lodge, where a loop track leads through the forest to limestone outcrops near Long Beach. From here the track leads down onto the dunes and back through the forest to the lodge. The round trip takes about two hours.

Cannon-Peirce and Harold Peirce Scenic Reserves: These two reserves (65 and 29 hectares respectively) are located at the northwest corner of Chatham Island. Both were gifted to the Crown in 1986 by Harold and Madeline Peirce, and feature remnant coastal forest. Of particular interest are a large number of ngaio, otherwise rare on the Chatham Islands. Access is by way of Waitangi West beach; visitors are advised to leave their vehicle at the road end and walk north along the beach to the mouth of Waihi Creek and along the northern boundary of the creek to the reserves.

The nationally endangered Chatham Island toetoe has been restored via plantings in Harold Peirce Scenic Reserve.

Colin Miskelly

Te Awatea Scenic Reserve: Te Awatea protects a 50-hectare remnant of rare swamp forest at the southeast corner of Lake Huro. The core reserve was surveyed off from the Te Awatea Farm Settlement in 1986, and an additional 4.5 hectares was gifted by Phil Seymour in 1998. The dominant trees are Chatham Island karamu, swamp akeake and matipo, along with the rarer Cox's matipo. Away from the lake the forest is dominated by kopi with scattered nikau and tarahinau. Access to and through the reserve is difficult, owing to the dense vegetation, high water table and the need to cross private land.

Te Awatea Scenic Reserve and Lake Huro.

Peter Johnson

Ocean Mail Scenic Reserve: The 830-hectare Ocean Mail property was purchased in 1990 and fenced shortly afterwards. The road to Kaingaroa passes through the reserve for about 5 kilometres, defined by cattlestops at each end.

Ocean Mail contains a variety of interesting habitats that are not well represented in other reserves. In the coastal margin the threatened Chatham Island sow thistle grows in the foredunes, and pingao (rare on the Chatham Islands) is present in scattered patches. Further back in the dunes the remnant akeake, kopi and matipo forest is starting to regenerate following years of browsing. South of the road the extensive wetland contains important populations of Chatham Island bamboo-rush, aster and speargrass, and is home to ducks, swans and pukeko.

Leaving vehicles at the roadside near the western cattlestop, visitors can follow a track south along the fenceline, beside Kaipakau

Kaingaroa and Te One School pupils planting Chatham Island akeake, aided by parents and DOC staff, Ocean Mail Scenic Reserve, June 2005.

Alex McKillop

Lake (Lake Wharemanu) to the shore of Te Whanga Lagoon. A new track loops back to the road, then through recent plantings of Chatham Island akeake to the coastal dunes, where there is a picnic shelter near the style. The plantings were undertaken by Kaingaroa and Te One school children, starting in 2003.

In 1994, fire ravaged 84 per cent of the reserve, leaving only the coastal-dune vegetation intact. The wetland vegetation has since recovered spectacularly.

Pitt Island scenic reserves

The three scenic reserves on Pitt Island were set aside for the protection of a range of forest and herbfield communities. The island has no possums or rats, and so some species rare or absent on Chatham Island thrive here (e.g. rautini and Chatham Island tomtit and tui). Access to the reserves requires crossing either private or leasehold land, and the appropriate owners must be contacted before a visit is made to the island.

The reserves were created and fenced during the 1970s after Jim Moffett agreed to reduce the area of his grazing lease before the land was purchased by the Crown. Herbert Preece contributed an adjacent 135-hectare block of forest, which was registered as the Frederick and Mary Hunt Memorial Conservation Covenant in 1999. The 100-hectare Meehan Conservation Covenant (Bill and Dianne Gregory-Hunt) immediately to the north was added in 2007.

Waipaua Scenic Reserve: This 692-hectare reserve and the adjoining Frederick and Mary Hunt Memorial Conservation Covenant and Meehan Conservation Covenant protect the central forest block of

Waipaua Scenic Reserve, central Pitt Island.

Peter Johnson

Canister Cove Scenic Reserve, southern Pitt Island.

John Marris

Pitt Island, providing important habitat for the endemic tomtit, tui, warbler, red-crowned parakeet and Barker's koromiko. The reserve and covenants also contain large numbers of the endemic rautini, which make a spectacular show of yellow flowers during summer, and the largest population of nikau remaining on the Chatham Islands. A population of feral Saxon merino sheep is maintained and hunted by Pitt Islanders, mainly in the southern half of the reserve and adjacent leasehold land. Wild pigs are also present in the reserve.

Canister Cove Scenic Reserve: Comprising the southern 615 hectares of Pitt Island, this reserve provides spectacular views of rugged coastlines, secluded harbours and offshore islands. The forest is largely tarahinau, with substantial numbers of hoho and Chatham Island karamu. Keketerehe grows in the south of the reserve. Regeneration is prolific, as most browsing animals were removed by the late 1970s, and the last feral sheep were shot in 1993. Bird diversity is similar to Waipaua, but numbers are lower because Canister Cove is more exposed to the prevailing winds.

Rangiauria Scenic Reserve: This immense basalt outcrop provides some of the best views on the Chatham Islands. The 41-hectare fenced reserve protects herbfield communities that include coxella and Chatham Island forget-me-not. Black-winged petrels have attempted to colonise Rangiauria, as attested by cat-killed corpses near the summit.

Conservation areas

'Conservation area' is a term used for land held for conservation purposes under the Conservation Act but not specifically declared a reserve under

Exposed western slopes at Rangiauria, Pitt Island. More than 60 metres above sea level, wind-blown salt enables iceplant (*Disphyma papillatum*) to grow among pasture grasses. Remnant akeake is visible in the foreground.

John Marris

the Reserves Act. There are nine such areas on the Chatham Islands, including the following four reserves on the main island. All were part of Wharekauri Station in central north Chatham Island, which was managed by the Department of Lands and Survey until 1987, during which time some reserves were created. The station then transferred to Landcorp (before being sold privately), with further areas of high conservation value set aside for management by DOC.

Nikau Bush Conservation Area: As its name suggests, this forest remnant features a stand of nikau palms, which are spectacular when in flower during December and January. The 17-hectare reserve was fenced in 1981 and regeneration has been prolific. A sign on North Road 2.5 kilometres south of the Wharekauri Road junction marks a carpark and the start of the access to the reserve (a 1-kilometre walk up the fenceline to the west). The round trip on the marked route takes about an hour.

Chudleigh Conservation Area: Situated on the southern flank of Mt Chudleigh, this 44-hectare reserve is readily visible from North Road, south of the Wharekauri Road junction (see page 85). The diverse forest remnant includes Chatham Island karamu, akeake, matipo and ribbonwood. As with other northern forest reserves, few endemic birds other than fantail are present.

Wharekauri (Green Swamp) Conservation Area: This 472-hectare reserve and the adjacent Green Swamp and Wharekauri Conservation Covenants together protect an extensive peat-swamp system, including rare swamp karamu/akeake forest. Notable endemic plants include Chatham Island aster, swamp karamu and extensive areas of bamboo-rush. The high

Fruiting nikau palms in the Nikau Bush Conservation Area.

Ian Flux, DOC

water table and dense inaka and bamboo-rush vegetation make the area easier to appreciate from a distance. A large fire destroyed 274 hectares of vegetation in the conservation area in late 2007.

Tangepu Conservation Area: Situated on the northern white-sand coast of Chatham Island, Tangepu provides an interesting day's visit and exploration possibilities. The 246-hectare reserve features remnant coastal vegetation, which is otherwise rare in this largely farmed part of the Chathams. Extending from the southern boundary of Lake Waikauia, the reserve includes about 4 kilometres of scenic coastline and provides habitat for the Chatham Island oystercatcher and threatened coastal plants, including pingao, coxella, shore spurge and Chatham Island sow thistle. Tangepu is about 4 kilometres from Wharekauri Road. To access the reserve, contact Wharekauri Station.

Covenants and Kawenata

Many Chatham Islanders have made a personal commitment to protecting their heritage through establishment of covenants on private land in conjunction with the Forest Heritage Fund, Nga Whenua Rahui, or directly with DOC. These schemes were established by the government in the early 1990s for the protection of important habitats. Under both schemes the land and its biota are protected by way of a covenant agreement between the landowner and the Minister of Conservation. Kawenata are covenants established on land owned by Moriori/Maori, using the Nga Whenua Rahui fund. The essence of most agreements is that the Minister of Conservation, through either of these funds, pays for fencing, survey and registration costs, while the landowner agrees to keep the land clear of browsing animals. These schemes have protected many sites that are important to the survival of threatened Chatham

The nationally vulnerable shore spurge (*Euphorbia glauca*) in the Tangepu Conservation Area.

Colin Miskelly

Islands species, including most endemic plant species, parea, and Chatham Island taiko, red-crowned parakeet, warbler, tomtit and tui.

There is insufficient space here to describe all of the 40 sites and their biodiversity values, although the principle landowners are recognised, along with the size of their covenants, in Chapter 11. However, in addition to the South Chatham Conservation Covenant (1200 hectares), Frederick and Mary Hunt Memorial Conservation Covenant (135 hectares), Meehan Conservation Covenant (100 hectares), and Green Swamp Conservation Covenant (99 hectares) mentioned above, three covenants stand out because of their large size or the high-profile species recovery work undertaken within them.

Kaingaroa Station Conservation Covenant: Established in 1995 by Barker Bros Ltd, the 247-hectare Kaingaroa Station Conservation Covenant includes the schist shore platform and dunes from just west of Okawa Point, past J. M. Barker (Hapupu) National Historic Reserve to the northeastern shore of Lake Kaingarahu. The covenant protects important duneland and coastal turf communities (see page 171), including the most extensive remaining stands of Chatham Island sow thistle, plus Chatham Island forget-me-not and the only pingao in Hanson Bay.

Sweetwater Conservation Covenant: Although small, the Sweetwater Conservation Covenant established in 2003 by Bruce and Liz Tuanui is an important site for two of the most endangered bird species on the

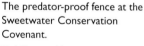

The predator-proof fence at the Sweetwater Conservation Covenant.

Toni Gregory-Hunt

Chatham Islands. Situated at the southwest corner of the Tuku Nature Reserve, the covenant covers a hilltop that is believed to have held a Chatham Island taiko breeding colony as recently as the 1930s. After sourcing money from the Biodiversity Condition Fund and the Lottery Grants Board, the Chatham Island Taiko Trust (www.taiko.org.nz) funded construction of a predator-proof fence around 2.5 hectares of the covenant in 2006, with the intention of attracting taiko and Chatham petrels to the site. All 21 known taiko chicks were moved to the covenant in April 2007 and 2008, and 47 Chatham petrel chicks were moved there in April 2008.

Ellen Elizabeth Preece (Caravan Bush) Conservation Covenant: This 53-hectare covenant near the east coast of Pitt Island was established in 1998 through an agreement with landowners John and Bridget Preece, and Greg and Karen Preece. A cat-proof fence enclosing 36 hectares of the covenant was built by DOC in 2001, specifically to provide additional habitat for black robin. Forty robins were translocated to the site between 2002 and 2005, but they failed to thrive, possibly owing to high numbers of mice competing for their insect food supply. The exclusion of cats, pigs and weka from most of the covenant has benefited the resident Chatham Island tomtit, tui, warbler and red-crowned parakeet populations, and provided suitable conditions for reintroduction of Chatham petrels in 2002–05 and Chatham Island snipe in 2008. By May 2008, 12 locally reared Chatham petrels had fledged from the covenant.

Little Mangere Island provided an impregnable fortress that protected the entire world populations of black robins and Forbes' parakeets for about 75 years.

Don Merton

Other important sites

Offshore islands

Many of the smaller offshore islands – often little more than rock stacks – are seabird-breeding sites of international importance. These include The Pyramid, Little Mangere Island, the Forty Fours and The Sisters. The importance of their plants and animals is recognised and valued by the islands' owners.

The Pyramid is the only breeding place for the Chatham Island mollymawk, with about 4200 pairs nesting annually. The Sisters and Forty Fours are nesting sites for about 6500 pairs of northern royal albatross, over 17,000 pairs of Pacific mollymawk, and about 2500 pairs of northern giant petrel. These albatross-nesting islands are also the strongholds for the threatened Chatham Island button-daisy.

Te Whanga Lagoon

More than 18,300 hectares in area, and open to the sea for much of the time, Te Whanga Lagoon has an abundance of marine life and is a major habitat for wading birds and waterfowl, especially black swans. The lagoon's eels, flounder, whitebait and cockles are valued as traditional food by Chatham Islanders. Swan eggs are harvested for food, and the birds themselves are hunted.

The coastline

The Chatham Islands coastline is spectacular and provides important habitat for birds and plants. Chatham Island and Pitt Island shags are often seen, and nest on cliffs and headlands. The endangered Chatham Island oystercatcher may be found around much of the coast, especially in the northwest and on Pitt Island. Blue penguins come ashore to breed all around the islands. The coastal cliffs, largely because of their inaccessibility to browsing animals, are refuges for many threatened plants, including Cook's scurvy grass, Chatham Island sow thistle and forget-me-not, and coxella.

Landowner permission must be obtained to access most coastal sites. Care should be taken not to disturb birds, especially when they are nesting. Oystercatcher nests high on the beach are particularly vulnerable to crushing by vehicles, which should be kept below the high-tide line.

The work

Implicit in all aspects of conservation work is the special relationship with tangata whenua and the need to work closely with the community, especially landowners. The Waitangi Tribunal settlement process is likely to lead to co-management of some sites, thus implementing the spirit of partnership explicit in the Treaty of Waitangi.

154

DOC's work on the Chatham Islands includes:

Habitat protection

Much effort goes into negotiating covenant agreements and preparing funding bids on behalf of landowners for the fencing of covenants and kawenata. New covenant fences are often built by landowners under contract to DOC. Departmental staff check, maintain and replace reserve and covenant fences.

A feral cat captured near nesting territories of Chatham Island oystercatchers, Chatham Island north coast.

Peter Moore

Biosecurity and pest control

A major focus of DOC's work on the Chatham Islands is on reducing or eliminating the harmful effects of introduced pests. This includes taking measures to prevent the spread of rodents, weeds and wildlife diseases to outlying islands, and controlling animal and plant pests that are adversely affecting threatened species or plant communities. Possum control is undertaken in many reserves and covenants on Chatham Island, and farm stock and feral stock are removed from these sites where necessary. Control of feral cats and introduced weka is mainly undertaken in the Tuku Nature Reserve and adjacent covenants to protect taiko and parea, and also at some coastal sites to protect nesting oystercatchers. Rats are controlled around active taiko burrows.

Weed control is undertaken to eliminate or contain invasive species with limited distributions on the islands (weed-led programmes), and to protect priority sites from the range of invasive species present there (site-led programmes). DOC also works with the Chatham Islands Council to reduce the risk of new invasive organisms reaching the islands, and to respond to incursions when they occur. Recent biosecurity incursion responses (some based on unconfirmed sightings) have included for rabbit, ferret, whistling frog, Chilean rhubarb (*Gunnera tinctoria*) and veldt grass (*Ehrharta erecta*).

A Chatham petrel burrow entrance protected with a neoprene (wetsuit material) screen. The petrels push through to access their egg or chick in the nest box at rear, but competing broad-billed prions are deterred by the screen. Rangatira Island.

Don Merton

Threatened species management

Activities undertaken to achieve threatened bird species recovery goals include nest-site location and protection, monitoring and translocations, and predator and competitor control. Recovery programmes are founded on detailed ecological research or well-designed management trials. Species that have been the focus of management and research over the last decade include Chatham Island taiko, oystercatcher, mollymawk and snipe, Chatham petrel, black robin, Forbes' parakeet, parea and shore plover. Monitoring of population trends has been undertaken for many other species, including Chatham Island shag, warbler, tomtit and red-crowned parakeet, brown skua, royal albatross, and Pitt Island shag. Threatened invertebrate recovery is largely achieved through the protection and restoration of their habitat, though some species are

DOC staff member Amanda Baird moved to the Chatham Islands in 1996, and has focused on threatened plant recovery programmes and habitat protection ever since. In 2007 she was awarded the Loder Cup for her plant conservation work.

Peter Moore

rarely recorded and poorly known despite targeted surveys (e.g. Pitt Island longhorn beetle, and *Thotmus* weevil).

More than 20 Chatham Islands plant species are considered threatened, and most of these occur only on the Chatham Islands. The main threats to plants are browsing by domestic and feral stock, pigs and possums, and competition from weeds. Some species dependent on disturbance and high nitrate levels have suffered following the decline or disappearance of seals and seabirds on the main islands. Threatened plant recovery actions include protecting existing populations and restoring plants to suitable sites where browsing mammals are excluded. DOC maintains a small nursery at Te One to propagate plants for both threatened species recovery programmes and site restoration projects (see page 107). Considerable success has been achieved through monitoring survival and growth of plantings made in different conditions, to guide subsequent plantings.

Ecological restoration

While small-scale plantings of threatened species are undertaken at many sites, more extensive plantings and weed control at selected sites help to restore lost or damaged plant communities. Notable among these are the restoration of forest to Mangere Island, community tree plantings at Ocean Mail Scenic Reserve, and restoration of coastal dune vegetation at Tioriori and Wharekauri on the north coast.

Visitors reading interpretation panels at the entrance to the J. M. Barker (Hapupu) National Historic Reserve.

Colin Miskelly

Provision of visitor information and facilities, and education

DOC maintains short walking tracks, interpretation panels and other visitor facilities in the more accessible reserves (Hapupu, Henga, Nikau Bush, Thomas Mohi Tuuta (Rangaika), and Ocean Mail), and also in the Ellen Elizabeth Preece Conservation Covenant on Pitt Island. A range of books and brochures on the islands is held at the Chatham Islands Area Office at Te One. DOC staff also work with the three schools (Te One, Kaingaroa and Pitt Island) to incorporate conservation themes in the curriculum and to involve pupils in conservation projects.

Managing historic sites

The New Zealand Historic Places Trust, a separate entity from DOC, has registered eight Chatham Islands buildings of historical importance. Only one of these (Glory Cottage on Pitt Island; see page 47) is managed by DOC, but many important archaeological sites are protected on reserves managed by the department. These include rakau momori (Moriori tree carvings), parahanga (midden sites), and remnants of early European sealing, whaling and farming industries.

Marine mammal strandings and fire suppression

Some situations require an urgent response that can be prepared for but not predicted. The Chatham Islands have a very high number of marine mammal strandings. Many thousands of whales have stranded and died on the islands over the years, with mass strandings of hundreds of pilot whales a common occurrence. Because of the islands' isolation and limited resources compared with mainland New Zealand, it is rarely possible to save these animals. Data are collected from stranded animals, along with tissue samples and skeletal remains of rare species. Where decaying carcasses present a health risk or nuisance, DOC is responsible for their removal or disposal.

DOC staff are trained in rural firefighting. In addition to issuing fire permits, staff respond to any fires threatening reserves and covenants.

Other work

Most field programmes have a significant office-based component, including preparing funding applications and proposals, and collating results and preparing reports on the outcomes of management trials. The results of threatened bird and plant recovery programmes are presented at annual recovery group meetings, usually held on Chatham Island. Reports are also presented to the Chatham Islands Conservation Board, an advisory body composed of community representatives and receiving administrative support from DOC. Support staff also facilitate fieldwork through a wide range of tasks, including organising purchase of field supplies and equipment, maintaining the vehicle fleet, and managing the planning and reporting systems required of government agencies.

PUBLIC ACCESS CODE OF CONDUCT

Access

Unrestricted public access is provided to scenic reserves, historic reserves and conservation areas administered by the Department of Conservation, but access to nature reserves is by permit only. Permission must always be obtained before entering or crossing private land, including access to many coastal areas. If in doubt, ask at the DOC office in Te One, or at the Chatham Islands Council office in Waitangi. DOC manages an informal camping area within Ocean Mail Scenic Reserve, but otherwise there are no camping facilities in DOC reserves, nor are horses or vehicles (including mountain bikes) permitted within them.

Respect

Visitors must remember that all plants, animals, and archaeological and historical sites within DOC reserves are protected. Removal of any material or leaving any rubbish is strictly prohibited. Take only photographs, leave only footprints. In many cases, what you see is unique to the Chatham Islands; it should be treated with respect. Extreme care must be taken with fire on and around reserves; fires are usually prohibited within reserves, and they always require a permit.

Introduced species

The Chatham Islands are free from many of the introduced pests (especially weeds) found in mainland New Zealand. Visitors should be aware of this and take care not to inadvertently introduce any alien species to the islands.

CHAPTER ELEVEN

PEOPLE WHO MADE A DIFFERENCE

Many people have contributed to the understanding and protection of the Chatham Islands' natural and historic heritage. The following brief biographies feature some of the key people who have made an enduring contribution.

Ernst Dieffenbach

Professor Johann Karl Ernst Dieffenbach (1811–55) was a German naturalist, geologist, ethnologist and writer who had a brief (1839–41) but influential stay in New Zealand. As surgeon and naturalist to the New Zealand Company, Dieffenbach was the first scientist to visit the Chathams, where he spent about 10 weeks in May–July 1840, based aboard the ship *Cuba*. In addition to describing the climate, geology and landforms of the islands, Dieffenbach described and collected plant, fish, bird and fossil-shell specimens, and noted that Norway rats, cats, dogs and pigs were present. Among the bird species he recorded or collected were parea (Chatham Island pigeon), shoveler duck, and Chatham Island red-crowned parakeet, bellbird, warbler and tomtit. He also collected the unique specimen of Dieffenbach's rail before it became extinct. A fossil deposit found by Dieffenbach on the north coast of Chatham Island is considered the first fossil locality described from New Zealand. His name is commemorated in the scientific names of the rail, coxella (Dieffenbach's speargrass) and Dieffenbach's koromiko.

Ernst Dieffenbach, 1843.

Detail from lithograph by Joseph Merrett, Alexander Turnbull Library, A-259-010

Top: **Department of Conservation staff landing on Rangatira Island Nature Reserve.** Don Merton

Henry Travers.

National Botanic Gardens, Glasnevin, Ireland

Chatham Island speargrass (*Aciphylla traversii*) was named after Henry Travers.

Geoff Walls

Henry Forbes.

Canterbury Museum, detail from 1977.2.1

Henry Travers

Henry Hammersley Travers (1844–1928) was a New Zealand-based scientific collector who visited the Chatham Islands for six months from October 1863, and again for six months from July 1871. Travers described the appearance and living conditions of Moriori, gave detail of landforms and plants, and collected many plant, bird, lizard, insect and rock specimens. The plant specimens were given to Baron Ferdinand von Mueller of Melbourne, and remain in the National Herbarium of Victoria. Mueller used specimens from Travers' 1863–64 visit in his 1864 book *The Vegetation of the Chatham Islands*, describing 87 species, including eight that were new (and overlooking several other endemic species that he considered identical to mainland forms).

On Travers' second trip he collected many more plants and examples of endemic bird species, including Chatham Island and Pitt Island shags, Chatham Island rail, oystercatcher, pigeon, fantail and tui, black robin and Forbes' parakeet, and the first Chatham Island specimens of shore plover. Travers also collected specimens of Chatham Island snipe and fernbird from Mangere Island, though both had previously been collected there in 1867 by visiting naturalist Charles Traill of Stewart Island. Of these species, the Chatham Island rail and fernbird are now extinct. Henry Travers' connection with the Chatham Islands is commemorated in the scientific names of the black robin, Chatham Island speargrass, Chatham Island bamboo-rush, spade-toothed whale (*Mesoplodon traversii*), a longhorn beetle (*Xylotoles traversi*), a weevil (*Inophloeus traversi*), a fossil scallop (*Tucetona traversi*) and a fossil brachiopod (lamp shell, *Chathamithyris traversi*). However, the Chatham Island geranium was named after Henry's father, William Travers (1819–1903), who sponsored Henry's collecting trips, and the Chatham Island akeake was named after both father and son.

Henry Forbes

Dr Henry Ogg Forbes (1851–1932) was director of the Canterbury Museum 1888–92, and visited the Chatham Islands, including Mangere Island, in January–February 1892. He collected large quantities of bird bones from dune deposits, and went on to publish eight scientific articles referring to the Chatham Islands and their birds, all during 1892–93. These included descriptions of the Chatham Island shag and four newly recognised extinct species: Hawkins' rail, a coot, a snipe (larger than the living Chatham Island snipe) and a raven. The rail was named after William Hawkins, a professional bird collector, who was Forbes' guide and assistant on the Chatham Islands. The enigmatic Chatham Island sea eagle, so beautifully illustrated in the first edition of this book, was described in 1973 based on about a dozen bones from four birds, labelled as collected on the Chatham Islands by Forbes. These bones are now believed to be modern bones, possibly from the Alaskan race of the bald eagle, and are very unlikely to have come from the Chatham Islands. In addition to the birds that he described and named, Forbes is also commemorated in Forbes' parakeet (*Cyanoramphus forbesi*).

Hugo Schauinsland

Professor Hugo Hermann Schauinsland (1857–1937) was the director of the Bremen Übersee-Museum 1896–1933. In the company of a colleague, Professor Johann Dietrich Alfken, he visited the Chatham Islands during January–February 1897 while travelling around the Pacific. Schauinsland was an energetic collector and took back to his native Germany a very wide range of animals and fossils from the Chathams. Many Chatham Islands terrestrial and marine invertebrates were named after him, including the magnificent but much-maligned Rangatira spider, a diving beetle (*Rhantus schauinslandi*), a marine sponge (*Leucandra schauinslandi*), a sea squirt (*Amphicarpa schauinslandi*), and a possibly endemic genus of parasitic wasp (*Schauinslandia*) with three named species from the Chatham Islands.

Hawkins' rail (*Diaphorapteryx hawkinsi*), named by Henry Forbes after his guide, William Hawkins.

Painting by Paul Martinson, Museum of New Zealand, Te Papa Tongarewa, MA_I043836

Far left: Hugo Schauinsland.
Übersee-Museum, Bremen

Left: Rangatira spider (*Dolomedes schauinslandi*) female carrying an egg sac. The species was collected by, and named after, Professor Hugo Schauinsland.
John Marris

Leonard Cockayne

Dr Leonard Cockayne (1855–1934) is considered the father of New Zealand plant ecology. He spent six weeks on Chatham Island in January–February 1901, and in 1902 published the ironically titled 82-page paper 'A Short Account of the Plant-covering of Chatham Island' in the *Transactions of the New Zealand Institute*. This detailed record set an invaluable benchmark for what Chatham Islands vegetation would have been like before much of the original pattern was altered by farming, browsing animals and the introduction of new plant species. In the paper Cockayne described five species that are still considered valid – tarahinau, Cox's matipo, and Chatham Island karamu, ribbonwood and kowhai. Cockayne went on to establish the Otari Open-air Native Plant Museum in Wellington. He received numerous awards and honours, including being appointed a Companion of the Most Distinguished Order of St Michael and St George (CMG) in 1929.

Leonard Cockayne, 1897.
Alexander Turnbull Library, detail from 056747

Thomas Hall

Thomas Hall (1876–1917) was an itinerant shepherd who worked on Pitt Island in the early 1900s, probably for Richard Paynter. In mid-1906 he was induced to start collecting insects by Edgar Waite, then curator of the Canterbury Museum, who visited Pitt Island. Hall, assisted by Robert Paynter, collected Pitt Island beetles through to January 1908, when he moved to Methven. The collection was forwarded to Major Thomas Broun, who published a paper based on the collection in 1911, listing 55 new beetle records from the Chathams and describing 28 as new species that are still recognised today. Before then, only 45 beetle species were known from the islands. Broun's Chatham Islands collection is housed in the Natural History Museum, London. In addition to finding the first specimens of the coxella weevil (*Hadramphus spinipennis*), Hall found the only known specimen of another large weevil (now known as *Thotmus halli*) while on Pitt Island. This is the only species described for the genus, which is endemic to the Chathams; the species has not been seen again and is probably extinct. Hall continued to collect large numbers of beetles from South Island sheep stations for Broun until 1916, when he enlisted in the New Zealand Rifle Brigade. He was killed in action in France on 20 August 1917.

The unique specimen of *Thotmus halli* (a weevil), collected by Thomas Hall on Pitt Island c.1907.
Max Barclay, Natural History Museum, London

Alexander Shand

Alexander Shand (1840–1910) arrived on the Chatham Islands as a 14-year-old in 1855, when his father started service as the islands' first Resident Magistrate and Collector of Customs. Shand worked as a sheep farmer but, after learning the Maori language from local Ngati Mutunga, also held the positions of Government Interpreter and clerk to the Resident Magistrate. He recognised the plight of the Moriori and was concerned that their language and culture would disappear without adequate documentation. Shand became absorbed in this project, learning the Moriori language and becoming the confidant of the few remaining full-blooded Moriori. He was considered the only scholar to be acquainted with Moriori language and traditions. Much of Alexander Shand's careful scholarship was preserved in his 1911 book *The Moriori People of the Chatham Islands: Their history and traditions*, but the completed final chapter and the supporting reference material were destroyed in a house fire that claimed Shand's life.

Alexander Shand.
Polynesian Society

Arthur Cox

Lieutenant Felix Arthur Douglas Cox (1837–1915) was an Englishman who served in the British Army in India before arriving in New

Zealand in 1863. He settled on the Chatham Islands in 1865, forming a longstanding partnership with his brother-in-law, Alexander Shand (see page 162). Together they farmed Whangamarino, between Lake Huro and Waitangi, until the lease expired two years after Shand's death. Cox was an enthusiastic naturalist, supplying plants and information to all the leading botanists of the time, including Thomas Kirk, Thomas Cheeseman, Donald Petrie and Leonard Cockayne. Cheeseman named the genus *Coxella* (for Dieffenbach's speargrass, now *Aciphylla dieffenbachii*) after him, noting: 'During a lengthened residence in this outlying corner of the Dominion Mr. Cox has regularly and consistently collected specimens of the flora of the islands. These he has communicated to most New Zealand botanists, accompanying them with much valuable information. It is largely through his assistance in supplying material that our present knowledge of the Chatham Islands florula is in such a satisfactory position.' Although the genus *Coxella* is no longer used, Cox's name persists in the endemic Chatham Island plants Cox's matipo and Cox's fescue, and in the common name of both coxella and the coxella weevil. Cox's daughter Daisy married Harry Blyth of Tuku farm, providing a link with Charles Fleming, David Crockett and Manuel Tuanui (see below).

Arthur Cox, c.1910.

Ernest Guest, Guest Collection, Alexander Turnbull Library, detail from PICT-000094

Charles Fleming

Sir Charles Alexander Fleming (1916–87) first visited Chatham Island as a schoolboy in 1933. He returned with fellow university student Graham Turbott in 1937, and they teamed up with Kaingaroa school teacher Allan Wotherspoon to investigate the birds of the Chatham Islands over the 1937–38 summer. Highlights included landing on The Pyramid, a fortnight camped on Rangatira Island studying shore plover, and a much-anticipated landing on Little Mangere Island on 2 January 1938, where they rediscovered the black robin and Forbes' parakeet.

Coxella weevil on coxella (Dieffenbach's speargrass); both common names commemorate Arthur Cox.

John Marris

Fleming's findings were published as 'Birds of the Chatham Islands' in the journal *Emu* in 1938.

Although employed as a geologist, Fleming remained a staunch advocate for bird conservation and research on the Chathams for the rest of his life. He lobbied for the purchase of Rangatira and Mangere Islands as reserves, and for support for the black robin recovery programme. He was a member of the New Zealand Fauna Protection Advisory Council and its predecessors almost continuously from 1955, often advising on Chatham Islands recovery programmes. He returned to the Chathams in 1977 as a guest of the Wildlife Service during the second transfer of black robins from Little Mangere Island to Mangere Island, and again in 1984 on a 'Fauna PAC' visit to Rangatira and Pitt Islands. Fleming's connection with the Chatham Islands is commemorated in the scientific names of a bivalve mollusc (*Austrotindaria flemingi*) and a deep-sea urchin (*Pseudoechinus flemingi*) collected from the Chatham Rise, reflecting his broad scientific interests. Recognition of Fleming's services to New Zealand science came with his appointment as an Officer of the Order of the British Empire (OBE) in 1964, and as a Knight Commander of the Order of the British Empire (KBE) in 1977.

Christina Jefferson

Christina Jefferson (c.1891–1974) of Waihi Beach, Bay of Plenty, undertook a landmark study of Moriori tree carvings (rakau momori) between 1947 and 1955. She spent over 16 months on the islands during her six visits, camping out alone much of the time and travelling over 1000 kilometres on horseback. Before her research it was thought that few tree carvings survived. Through detailed surveys, Jefferson found 1145 carvings, and photographed or made pencil copies of 549 of them. Her findings were published in the *Journal of the Polynesian Society*

and reprinted as a book, *Dendroglyphs of the Chatham Islands: Moriori designs on karaka trees* (1956). Jefferson departed the islands under controversy over disturbance of koiwi (bones of Moriori ancestors). Apart from two brief notes on burial customs of the Moriori and a Moriori playing bowl published in the *Journal of the Polynesian Society* in 1949, Jefferson apparently did not undertake any other anthropological research.

Brian Bell

Brian Douglas Bell joined the Wildlife Branch of Internal Affairs as a senior field officer in 1957, and first visited the Chatham Islands (with Ian Hogarth) in September 1961. (The Wildlife Branch became the Wildlife Service in 1974, and was incorporated in the newly formed Department of Conservation in 1987.) The two men spent two weeks on South East Island Flora & Fauna Reserve (as it was then known), where they shot the last 14 sheep. They then visited Mangere Island (then still farmed), and climbed Little Mangere Island for the first time since Fleming in 1938, after which Bell recommended that black robins be translocated to South East Island. This eventually happened in 1983. Bell recognised the potential of Mangere Island as a reserve and was the key figure in lobbying for its purchase and negotiating removal of the sheep. He led a larger team to the Chathams in 1968, when he and Don Merton shot the remaining sheep on Mangere Island, which had been purchased in 1966. Bell also recommended that black robins be moved there. Bell and Merton initiated the agreement for P. Feron and Son Ltd to sell southern Pitt Island to the Crown in 1973, and Bell negotiated the eventual scenic reserve boundaries with the then leaseholder, Jim Moffett.

Brian Bell and Don Merton looking for sheep on Mangere Island, 1968.

John Kendrick, DOC

Bell embodied the Wildlife Service attitude of taking direct action and of never giving up on endangered species, no matter how overwhelming the odds. This contributed to the service's international reputation for effective species management and island pest eradications. He remained closely involved in Chatham Islands threatened bird management from his next visit, in 1973, through to 1992, including leading the teams that transferred all seven surviving black robins from Little Mangere to Mangere Island 1976–77. Bell's connection with Chatham Islands conservation continued throughout the employment of his son Mike by DOC there 1995–98, and subsequent contract field work undertaken by Mike and his siblings Dave, Elizabeth, Paul and Philip Bell. Brian Bell was a contributing author to the first edition of this book. He received the Queen's Service Medal (QSM) for public service in 1984, and currently manages a conservation consultancy company based in Blenheim.

Brian Bell and Don Merton about to release black robins on Pitt Island, 2002.

Don Merton

Don Merton

Dr Donald Vincent Merton made the first of his 31 trips to the Chatham Islands as a senior fauna conservation officer for the Wildlife Branch in 1968. He was closely involved with the research programme on black robins on Little Mangere Island 1972–76, then became the key figure during the intensive management of the robins 1976–89, when black robins were transferred first to Mangere Island then to Rangatira, and their numbers increased from five to over 80 birds. During this time Merton developed and modified many techniques not previously used on small songbirds, including cross-fostering, and safe methods to move eggs, chicks and adults between islands on local fishing boats, often in rough seas. Merton shifted focus to DOC's kakapo recovery programme during the 1990s, but returned to Chatham Islands to experience the dawn of the new millennium from the summit of Rangatira. He also participated in the transfers of black robins from Rangatira to Pitt Island in 2002 and 2004, before retiring from the department in 2005. Merton received a QSM for public service in 1989, and an honorary Doctor of Science degree from Massey University in 1992.

David Crockett with the first two taiko captured on 1 January 1978.

Russell Thomas

David Crockett

David Edgar Crockett joined the Ornithological Society of New Zealand (OSNZ) as a schoolboy in 1950. Through Ron Scarlett at the Canterbury Museum, and Charles Fleming, Crockett developed an interest in the mysterious taiko of the Chatham Islands, and corresponded with former Tuku landowner Harry Blyth in 1952. He first visited the Chatham Islands in 1969 and started dedicated searches for the taiko in 1972, culminating in the capture of two birds on the night of 1 January 1978. Crockett's 'Taiko Expeditions' maintains Taiko

Camp on land owned by the Tuanui family; it has been used as a base for 29 expeditions since 1972. Crockett and his teams of OSNZ volunteers and other taiko expeditioners continue to work closely with DOC during telemetry programmes every second year, when taiko are radio-tracked in order to locate further breeding burrows. Crockett lives in Whangarei and was a science educator before retiring in 1995. He is a foundation member of both the Chatham Island Taiko Trust (www.taiko.org.nz) and the Taiko Recovery Group, and has become a well-known identity on Chatham Island during his 62 visits over 39 years. Crockett was appointed a Companion of the Queen's Service Order (QSO) for public service in 2000.

Manuel and Evelyn Tuanui

Manuel Tuanui (1927–84) worked as a farmhand for Harry Blyth before purchasing his Tuku farm in 1956. Manuel and Evelyn and their family were enthusiastic supporters of the attempts by David Crockett and his team to rediscover the taiko, allowing search teams to camp on their land and providing much logistical support and encouragement. They were delighted by the capture of the first two taiko in 1978. In 1983 they generously donated the 1239-hectare Tuku Nature Reserve to the people of New Zealand, to protect the forest and the likely breeding site of the taiko. The first taiko burrow was found in 1987; about 80 per cent of known taiko breeding burrows are located within the Tuku Nature Reserve, which also holds the bulk of the world's parea population. Manuel Tuanui is commemorated in the scientific name of the Chatham redcoat damselfly (*Xanthocnemis tuanuii*).

Evelyn Tuanui holding a taiko at Taiko Camp, 1982.

Reg Cotter

Far left: Manuel Tuanui at Taiko Camp, 1982.

Stella Rowe

Left: Chatham redcoat damselfly (*Xanthocnemis tuanuii*), named after Manuel Tuanui.

Sönke Hardersen

David Given

Dr David Roger Given (1943–2005) was a botanist who made a life long contribution to plant conservation both nationally and globally. He made the first of many visits to the Chatham Islands in 1982 while employed by the Botany Division of the Department of Scientific and

David Given.
Karina Given

Michael King.
Dominion Post Collection, Alexander
Turnbull Library, EP-1992-3859-15

Industrial Research (DSIR). His association with the islands continued through to 2005 when, as a self-employed consultant, he was part of a multidisciplinary team researching the age, origin and evolution of the Chatham Islands and their biota. Many of Given's published works touched on the threatened plants of the Chatham Islands. Notable among these was *Rare and Endangered Plants of New Zealand* (1981), where his beautiful photographs and text brought the plight of 18 endemic Chatham plant species to a wide audience. He also included 11 Chatham plant species (eight endemic) in *The Red Data Book of New Zealand: Rare and endangered species of endemic terrestrial vertebrates and vascular plants* (1981; compiled with Gordon Williams), and 12 species in *Threatened Plants of New Zealand* (1989; co-authored with Catherine Wilson). Given's 1984 DSIR report *Conservation of Chatham Island Flora and Vegetation*, co-authored with Peter Williams, provided a solid foundation for ongoing conservation programmes. Given was a contributing author to the first edition of this book.

Michael King

Dr Michael King (1945–2004) was a widely respected historian and prolific writer. He first visited the Chatham Islands in 1986 to attend the unveiling of Tommy Solomon's statue at Manukau. Many visits followed during the research and writing of his two books on the Chatham Islands and their people: *Moriori: A people rediscovered* (1989), and *A Land Apart: The Chatham Islands of New Zealand* (1990, with photographer Robin Morrison). King was a member of the Chatham Islands Conservation Board 1990–93, and also acted as a guide for cultural and historical tours of the islands. Through his scholarship and writing, King had a major role in the cultural renaissance of the Moriori and was greatly looking forward to attending the opening of their Kopinga Marae in January 2005. His tragic death prevented this. King received many awards and fellowships for his research and writing, including an OBE for services to New Zealand literature in 1988.

David Holmes

David Livingstone Holmes (1906–2001) arrived on the Chatham Islands as a 16-year-old in 1922, when his father started service as the islands' sole constable. His busy life included working as a farmer, carrier and potato grower, and he served on the Chatham Islands Council for nearly 50 years, 14 of them as chairman. He never owned a motor vehicle and is rumoured to have retired when his last horse died. Holmes was widely respected as the foremost Chatham Islands historian of his generation, and he had a remarkable ability to recall details about people, places, dates and events. His unsurpassed knowledge was sought by many other researchers and was cheerfully shared, along with his generous hospitality, and that of his wife Joyce, at their stately 1880s Nairn House near Waitangi. Holmes' recollections were also published in his own book, *My Seventy Years on the Chatham Islands*, in 1993. Holmes was appointed as a Member of the Order of the British Empire (MBE) for services to the Chatham Islands in 1964, and as a Commander of the Order of the British Empire (CBE) in 1992.

David Holmes at his CBE investiture, 1992.

Robert & Jan Holmes

Chatham Island and Pitt Island landowners

Many Chatham Islanders have become concerned at the loss of their natural heritage, exemplified by the reduction in forest cover within their own lifetimes. Chatham Island and Pitt Island forests decline rapidly if farm stock have access, and this is exacerbated by the effects of feral stock and pigs, possum browse, fire and wind. The main solution to reverse the decline is to fence out farm stock and exclude feral stock. Some landowners have taken this initiative at their own cost, or have gifted land as reserves. Others have entered into covenant agreements with the Department of Conservation, with the land remaining in freehold title, while fencing costs are met by the government (mainly through the Forest Heritage Fund and Nga Whenua Rahui, with the latter fund established specifically to protect forests held in Maori title). Other DOC-funded fencing has occurred on private land to secure the boundaries of coastal reserves against wandering stock, while also protecting inherent flora and fauna values. Through these processes, several thousand hectares of Chatham Island and Pitt Island forests have been protected.

The most significant gifts of land as reserves have been: Thomas Mohi Tuuta (Rangaika) Scenic Reserve (407ha) by Thomas and Annie Tuuta in 1977; J. M. Barker (Hapupu) National Historic Reserve (29ha) by Barker Bros Ltd in 1979; Henga Scenic Reserve (170ha) by John and

Thomas Mohi Tuuta (Rangaika) Scenic Reserve, coastal slopes.

Amanda Baird

Tuku-a-tamatea River, Tuku
Nature Reserve.

Ian Cooksley

Denise Sutherland in 1981; Taia Bush Historic Reserve (34ha) by Sunday and Elsie Hough in 1981; Tuku Nature Reserve (1239ha) by Manuel and Evelyn Tuanui in 1983; Cannon-Peirce (60ha) and Harold Peirce (29ha) Scenic Reserves by Harold and Madeline Peirce in 1986; and Te Awatea Scenic Reserve addition (4.5ha) by Phil Seymour in 1998.

There are currently about 40 conservation covenants, kawenata and protected land management agreements on Chatham and Pitt Islands, totalling nearly 3000 hectares. The identified owners were those at the time that protection was agreed. Some land units are in multiple title, and only principle owners are identified here: Lake Huro Conservation Covenant (9.3ha), Pat and Wendy Smith 1983; Te Awapatiki & Wairoa Bush Kawenata (18.1ha), Alfred and Robyn Preece 1994; Tennants Lake Kawenata (16.8ha), Eric Dix 1994; Otonga Kawenata (23ha), Henry Daymond 1994; Nuhaka Kawenata (8.5ha), Tom Lanauze 1994; Rapanui Kawenata (86ha), Bob Goomes 1994; Te One School Kawenata (4.5ha), Bob Goomes 1994; Tuuta Kawenata (8.9ha), Albert Tuuta 1994; Mairangi Conservation Covenant (12.6ha), Keith Kamo, and Leo, Donald and Albert Tuuta 1995; Te Roto Conservation Covenant (6.1ha), Raana Tuuta 1995; Kaingaroa Station Conservation Covenant (247ha), Stephen and Celia Barker, and Thomas Anderson 1995; Frederick and Mary Hunt Memorial Conservation Covenant (135ha), Pitt Island,

John and Bridget Preece 1998; Ellen Elizabeth Preece (Caravan Bush) Conservation Covenant (53ha), Pitt Island, John and Bridget Preece, and Greg and Karen Preece 1998; Tuku Conservation Covenant (52ha), Bruce and Liz Tuanui 1999; Awatotara Manuel and Evelyn Tuanui Family Conservation Covenant (70ha), Bruce Tuanui 1999; Gillespie Creek Conservation Covenant (72ha), Alfred and Robyn Preece 1999; Big Bush Conservation Covenant (6.4ha), Raana Tuuta 2000; Frank's Bush Conservation Covenant (70ha), Greg and Rosemarie Horler 2001; Matakatau Creek Conservation Covenant (28ha), Denis Prendeville and Debra Whittaker-Prendeville 2001; Otauwe Point Conservation Covenant (25ha), Ron Seymour 2001; Rakautahi Conservation Covenant (9.1ha), Alison Turner and Simon Norman 2002; Te Matarae Conservation Covenant (12.3ha), P. and W. Smith Family Trust 2002; Owenga Kawenata (70ha), Rangaika Kawenata (c.164ha) and Owenga

Dune vegetation, Kaingaroa Station Conservation Covenant. Prostrate sand coprosma (*Coprosma acerosa*) in the foreground, and dune mingimingi (*Leucopogon parviflorus*).

Colin Miskelly

East Kawenata (c.45ha), Alfred and Robyn Preece 2002; Sweetwater Conservation Covenant (6.7ha), Bruce and Liz Tuanui 2003; Kiringe, Waterfall Bush and Waterfall Coast Conservation Covenants (23ha), Bruce and Liz Tuanui 2003; Rangitihi Conservation Covenant (69ha), Clifford and Eileen Whaitiri 2004; Waihi Conservation Covenant (15.2ha), Pat and Terry Tuanui 2005; Maunganui Conservation Covenant (14.5ha), Pat and Terry Tuanui, and Deirdre Thomas 2005; Green Swamp Conservation Covenant (99ha), Pat and Terry Tuanui, and Deirdre Thomas 2005; Wharekauri Conservation Covenant (5ha), Tony Anderson, Murray and Gillian Dix 2005; S. W. and E. F. Hough (Kakariki) Kawenata (65ha), Margaret Wyatt, Charles and Donald Hough 2005; Point Munning Conservation Covenant (47ha), Jim and Ben Muirson 2007; Waihora Conservation Covenant (2.9ha), Gary and Eileen Cameron 2007; Meehan Conservation Covenant (100ha), Pitt Island, Bill and Dianne Gregory-Hunt in progress; and South Chatham Conservation Covenant (1200ha), Ron Seymour, Robert and Jan Holmes, Neville Day, and Chris Clark in progress.

Private land has also been fenced off to protect coastal reserve areas where stock would otherwise gain access from neighbouring banks or dunes, and to protect their inherent values: Tioriori to Tutuiri (13ha), Tuanui Bros; Lake Waikauia (8ha), Diknee Fleming; and Matarakau (13ha), Goomes family. A few landowners have fenced off substantial areas of forest and coastline at their own cost, e.g. about 240 hectares on the northern flanks of Hakepa and northeast coast of Pitt Island by James Moffett.

The Chatham Islands are a national and international treasure. Our knowledge of their natural and cultural heritage has developed over two brief centuries, passing through phases of exploration, colonisation, exploitation and co-existence that mirrored the pattern of European and Maori contact. Chatham Islanders have long valued their quality of life, self-sufficiency and communal strength, much of which was built around their sense of place on these rugged, beautiful islands surrounded by bounteous but often stormy seas. It is now easier for the islanders to understand the significance of their environment, as improved transport and communication allows comparison with the rest of the world. Perhaps it is this greater awareness, combined with the sense of loss of endemic species, untamed landscapes and cultural heritage, that has led to the huge increase in individual commitment to conservation over the last two or three decades. As long as the community and central and local government recognise the importance of the islands' natural values and historic heritage, there are no excuses for further losses. And there is growing confidence that many species can be returned to sites where they can be seen and appreciated by islanders and their guests.

FURTHER READING

Aikman, H. and Miskelly, C. 2004. *Birds of the Chatham Islands*. Wellington, Department of Conservation.

Ballance, A. 2007. *Don Merton: The man who saved the black robin*. Auckland, Reed.

Butler, D. and Merton, D. 1992. *The Black Robin: Saving the world's most endangered bird*. Auckland, Oxford University Press.

Crisp, P., Miskelly, C. and Sawyer, J. 2000. *Endemic Plants of the Chatham Islands*. Wellington, Department of Conservation.

Campbell, H. and Hutching, G. 2007. *In Search of Ancient New Zealand*. Rosedale (New Zealand), Penguin Books and GNS Science.

Cemmick, R. and Veitch, D. 1985. *Black Robin Country*. Auckland, Hodder & Stoughton.

de Lange, P. J., Sawyer, J. W. D. and Ansell, R. 1999. *Checklist of Indigenous Vascular Plant Species Recorded from Chatham Islands*. Wellington, Department of Conservation.

Holdaway, R. N. (ed.) 1994. *Chatham Islands Ornithology*. Supplement to *Notornis* Vol. 41.

Holmes, D. 1993. *My Seventy Years on the Chatham Islands: Reminiscences*. Christchurch, Shoal Bay Press.

King, M. 1989. *Moriori: A people rediscovered*. Auckland, Viking.

King, M. and Morrison, R. 1990. *A Land Apart: The Chatham Islands of New Zealand*. Auckland, Random Century.

Lawrie, C. and Powell, J. 2006. *Discover the Chatham Islands: First to see the sun*. Berowra Heights, NSW, Australia, Deerubbin Press.

Miskelly, C. M., Bester, A. J. and Bell, M. 2006. Additions to the Chatham Islands' bird list, with further records of vagrant and colonising bird species. *Notornis* Vol. 53: pp. 213–28.

Richards, R. 1982. *Whaling and Sealing at the Chatham Islands*. Canberra, Roebuck Society.

Richards, R. 2007. *Manu Moriori: Human and bird carvings on live kopi trees on the Chatham Islands*. Wellington, Paremata Press.

Tennyson, A. and Martinson, P. 2006. *Extinct Birds of New Zealand*. Wellington, Te Papa Press.

Walls, G. 2002. *Unwanted Pests: Biosecurity threats to the Chatham Islands*. Wellington, Department of Conservation.

Walls, G., Baird, A., de Lange, P. and Sawyer, J. 2003. *Threatened Plants of the Chatham Islands*. Wellington, Department of Conservation.

Top: Sunrise. Helen Gummer

CONTRIBUTORS

Te Miria Kate Wills-Johnson (1929–95) was a fourth-generation Chatham Island descendant of early European settler Joe Dix. She spent much time and effort researching the history of Chatham Islands families from the first days of settlement. This led to the publication of her book *The People of the Chathams* (co-written with her husband, Gordon Wills-Johnson).

Michael King (1945–2004) was a historian who wrote over 30 books, including two on the Chatham Islands: *Moriori: A people rediscovered* and *A Land Apart: The Chatham Islands of New Zealand* (the latter with Robin Morrison). He was a member of the Chatham Islands Conservation Board 1990–93, and acted as a tour guide for cultural and historical tours of the islands. In 1988 he was awarded the OBE for services to New Zealand literature. The *New Zealand Herald* named him New Zealander of the Year for 2003. See page 168.

Hamish Campbell is a geologist with GNS Science, Lower Hutt, and is also the geologist at Te Papa. He first visited the Chatham Islands as part of the University of Otago archaeological expedition of 1975–76, to determine the sources of stone materials used by Moriori. This resulted in an abiding attachment to the islands, and a new geological map of the Chathams published in 1994. Hamish was co-leader of a 2004–07 research project exploring the origin and antiquity of the land surface in the Chatham Islands. He has also led tourist groups to the Chathams since 2002.

David Schiel is a marine biologist and ecologist. Formerly a scientist with the Ministry of Agriculture and Fisheries working on abalone (paua) and aquaculture, he is now Professor of Marine Science at the University of Canterbury. He and the Marine Ecology Research Group study a wide range of coastal problems relating to human impacts, functioning and resilience of coastal ecosystems.

Rhys Richards wrote an MA thesis titled 'An Historical Geography of Chatham Island' (1961), including maps of early vegetation. In 1982 he wrote 'A Tentative Population Map of Moriori on Chatham Island c.1791' (*Journal of the Polynesian Society*). Other publications include *Whaling and Sealing at the Chatham Islands* (1982), *Frederick Hunt of Pitt Island* (1990), *Murihiku Re-viewed* (1995), and *Manu Moriori: Human and bird carvings on live kopi trees on the Chatham Islands* (2007).

Ian Atkinson spent much of his scientific career studying ecological problems on islands. He first visited the Chathams in 1973 to find out why the forest on Little Mangere Island was collapsing, and in 1984 was part of a team looking at possible effects of proposed peat mining. He was a member of the Chatham Islands Conservation Board 1990–99.

Peter Johnson is a botanist, and is a research associate with Landcare Research in Dunedin. He was a member of the Chatham Islands Conservation Board 1999–2008, and leads botanical tours to the islands. He has written books on New Zealand wetland plants, and wetland types, and is currently preparing a handbook on wetlands of the Chatham Islands.

Peter de Lange is a threatened plant scientist with the Department of Conservation. Author of over a hundred papers on plant taxonomy and ecology, and eight books, he developed an interest in the Chatham Islands flora on his first visit there in 1996. He is currently writing a vascular plant flora of the islands, as well as researching its liverworts and mosses.

Peter Heenan is a botanist at the Allan Herbarium, Landcare Research at Lincoln. His research interests in the flora of the Chatham Islands include naturalised species and the taxonomy, phylogeny and biogeography of endemic species.

John Sawyer is a plant ecologist with the Department of Conservation in Wellington. He has co authored several books and reports about the flora of the Chatham Islands. He is member of the Chatham Plant Advisory Group, and works as part of this team on threatened plant protection, habitat restoration, biosecurity and weed programmes on the Chathams.

John Dugdale worked as an entomologist with Forest Research Institute and DSIR Entomology Division (later Landcare Research) until his retirement in 1995. He is an authority on butterflies, moths and cicadas, as well as tachinids (parasitic flies), and has been interested in Chatham Islands insects since 1967, when he went on Entomology Division's first expedition there. He subsequently visited the islands in 1988 and the early 1990s.

Rowan Emberson is an entomologist who was on the staff at Lincoln University from 1968 until he retired in 2002. His interest in island faunas and biogeography has taken him to the Chatham Islands on many occasions to study the insects. He has a particular interest in the beetle fauna, and the conservation of rare and endangered species.

Allan Munn's association with the Chatham Islands goes back to 1979 when he planted trees on Mangere Island for the Wildlife Service. He also worked on the black robin project, and was Field Centre Manager for the Department of Conservation on the Chatham Islands 1990–95. Allan was project manager and editor of the first edition of this book. He now farms near Hastings.

Ken Hunt has worked for the Department of Conservation since its inception in 1987, with extensive periods based at Taumarunui (working in Whanganui National Park) and latterly as manager of the Hawke's Bay Area. He has been Chatham Islands area manager since February 2007.

Colin Miskelly works for the Department of Conservation, based in Wellington. He first visited the Chatham Islands as a volunteer with Taiko Expeditions in 1978, then undertook thesis research on snipe on Rangatira between 1983 and 1986. He has been involved with conservation work on the Chatham Islands since 1998, visiting several times a year. He was co-author of the books *Endemic Plants of the Chatham Islands* and *Birds of the Chatham Islands*, and has published many technical articles on the ecology and conservation of Chatham Islands birds.

GLOSSARY

alkali feldspar	A subgroup of the feldspars, a major rock-forming group of minerals; potassium-sodium-aluminium silicate minerals [$KAlSi_3O_8$–$NaAlSi_3O_8$]
allopatric	Referring to species (or taxa) that have ranges that do not overlap (e.g. two related species each confined to a different island group). The opposite is 'sympatric'
argillite	Fine-grained sedimentary rock including siltstone and/or mudstone; commonly associated with greywacke, which is generally coarser-grained sandstone
Australasia	Collective term for Australia, New Guinea and New Zealand and immediate outlying islands, including New Caledonia. In practice used by most biogeographers to refer to Australia and New Zealand only
authigenic mineral	A mineral that has originated or crystallised (grown) *in situ*, i.e. where it occurs
baleen	Comb-like, flexible fibrous plates attached to the upper jaw in some whales, used to sieve small food items from seawater. Also known as 'whalebone', baleen was used to make a variety of fashion objects in the 1800s, including corset stays, umbrella ribs and hoops for skirts
basalt	A dark-coloured volcanic rock; the most common type of volcanic rock, and a major constituent of the oceanic crust
basement rock	The hardest and/or oldest rock upon which younger sediments and volcanic rocks have accumulated
biogenic mineral	Mineral material of biological origin; this includes common shell-forming minerals such as calcite and aragonite, and other minerals such as teeth-forming fluorapatite, and biogenic silica
biogeography	The study of distribution patterns of biota
biota	All living things at a site: plants, animals, fungi and microorganisms
bivalve mollusc	A mollusc with a shell composed of two hinged parts, e.g. a mussel, scallop or oyster
brachiopod	Shelled marine organisms, commonly known as lamp shells; filter-feeding animals with a hinged double, asymmetrical calcareous shell; similar to but unrelated to mollusc shells
brackish	A mixture of fresh and salt water typically found in upper estuaries and river mouths under tidal influence
bryozoan	A major group of sessile, colonial, filter-feeding marine animals ('bryozoa' means moss animal) that form a calcite skeleton; they form diverse shapes: clumps, bushes, laces, nets and sticks, but are best known as the plant-like fouling organisms on piers and the undersides of boats
calcareous	A rock or biogenic product (e.g. a shell) that is rich in calcium; in practice almost exclusively used for substrates and objects rich in calcium carbonate, such as limestone, calcareous siltstone, coralline algae, and mollusc shells

calcified	Having calcium carbonate in or on cell walls, forming a hard protective layer or covering
calcite	A stable form of calcium carbonate
calcium carbonate	A substance ($CaCO_3$) formed by chemical combination of calcium (Ca) with carbon dioxide (CO_2)
caldera	A large basin-shaped depression formed by the collapse of a volcano during or after an explosive eruption
carbonate	A substance formed by chemical combination with carbon dioxide (CO_3^2)
carbonised	A substance that has been burnt or oxidised to such an extent that all that is left appears to be carbon (C)
Cenozoic	A major subdivision of geological time that includes the Paleogene and Neogene Periods encompassing the last 65 million years
chiton	A limpet-like mollusc with eight hard plates on the top surface, generally found on rocky shores
conifer	A major division of the plants that includes all cone-bearing plants
conservation covenant	A formal agreement to protect freehold land for conservation purposes, registered on the title, where the land remains in private ownership. Survey and fencing costs are met by the Nature Heritage Fund
continental shelf	The submerged seabed from the edge of the coastline to the outer edge of the continental slope, generally less than 200 metres depth
covenant	*see* Conservation covenant
Cretaceous	A 'period'; a formal subdivision of geological time spanning 80.5 million years from 145.5 to 65.0 million years ago
crustose	A crust-like layer of algae or lichens flattened along a surface; commonly used for coralline algae that spread along rocky surfaces
cyanobacterium	From *cyanos* meaning blue; the term is widely used for photosynthetic bacteria, some of which are blue or blue-green in colour
detritivore	An invertebrate that feeds on dead and decaying plant material
disjunct	Biogeographical term used for a species that occurs in two or more widely separated populations
divaricating	Plants that exhibit an extremely angular, interlacing branching pattern, usually with the foliage, flowers and fruit held within the branchlets rather than at the ends. Such plants often have small leaves or no leaves
DNA	Deoxyribonucleic acid: a complex molecule that retains genetic information used for the construction of proteins in all known life forms
dyke	A subvertical body of rock, normally igneous, that is usually thin (measurable in centimetres to metres) and parallel-sided, that cuts or intrudes a pre-existing body of rock
endemic	Restricted to a particular geographical area; e.g. Chatham Island forget-me-not (*Myosotidium hortensia*) is endemic to the Chatham Islands, and does not occur naturally anywhere else in the world (cf. indigenous)
Eocene	An 'epoch'; a formal subdivision of the Paleogene Period of geological time, spanning 21.8 million years, from 55.5 to 33.7 million years ago

epicentre	The point on the Earth's surface directly above an earthquake source (hypocentre)
epiphyte	A plant that grows on another plant but is not parasitic on it
ethnology	A branch of anthropology dealing with races of people, their origins and characteristics
fault (geological)	A major fracture or dislocation along which the crust has moved
feldspar	A major rock-forming mineral group; a potassium-sodium-calcium-aluminium silicate mineral group ($KAlSi_3O_8$–$NaAlSi_3O_8$–$CaAl_2Si_2O_8$); the most common mineral type in crustal rocks
fen	Peatland receiving water and nutrients from adjacent mineral soils and therefore of low to moderate nutrient fertility and acidity
filamentous	Used to refer to algae that are thread-like or stringy
flora	A word with two meanings: a collective term for the plants of a particular region, or a compendium of written information about the plants of a particular area
fluorapatite	A fluorine-bearing calcium phosphate mineral and common mineral constituent of teeth
foliose	Having a leaf-like appearance, used in describing algae and lichens
foraminifera	A major group of single-celled marine animals, many of which secrete a calcareous (calcite) test or skeleton
genus (plural *genera*)	First word of a scientific name, used to group closely related species. For example, black robin and tomtit both belong to the genus *Petroica*
glauconite	A distinctive green authigenic potassium-bearing mineral that forms on the sea floor; the main mineral constituent of 'greensand'
Gondwanaland	The name given to a major landmass that existed during much of Mesozoic time; the name is derived from a region of eastern India with a distinctive succession of rock formations known as the 'Gondwana sequence'; Gondwanaland means 'land of Gondwana sequences' and includes India, Africa, South America, Australia, Antarctica and Zealandia
greywacke	A sedimentary rock that has been weakly to moderately metamorphosed; the original sediment was a muddy or silty sandstone; the most widespread Paleozoic to Mesozoic 'basement' rock in New Zealand
guano	Bird (or bat) faecal matter, especially where this accumulates in large deposits
half-graben	A depression (graben or valley) within the Earth's crust that develops adjacent to a normal fault after stretching or extension of the crust
hokairo manu	Traditional Moriori rock carvings
Holocene	An 'epoch'; a formal subdivision of the Neogene Period of geological time, encompassing the last 10,000 years
hornblende	A major group of rock-forming alumino-silicate minerals; a black, hydrated calcium-magnesium-iron-aluminium silicate mineral ($Ca_2(Mg,Fe,Al)_5(Al,Si)_8O_{22}(OH)_2$)
hornwort	A member of a group of prostrate liverwort-like plants with usually dark

green, often blue-green plate-like thalli (leaf-like structures), and light green wire-like, often curved fruiting bodies that rise above the thallus and have a superficial resemblance to horns (hence 'hornwort')

humus	Dark brown to black well-decomposed organic matter in soil, or suspended in water
hybrid swarm	A situation that arises when there is repeated hybridism between species that produce fertile hybrid progeny, and so are able to breed with other hybrids and their parents. The result is an often bewildering range of forms showing all gradations between the two parent species
imi	Moriori word for tribe
indigenous	Native to a country. In practice indigenous is usually segregated to refer to those life-forms found naturally within a particular region but which are also natural to other parts of the world (cf. endemic), e.g. silver fern (*Cyathea dealbata*) is indigenous to Chatham Island but it is also indigenous to the North and South Islands
intertidal	The area between the high- and low-tide marks that is exposed during low tide
introgression (genetics)	The movement of genes from one species into the gene pool of another, by backcrossing a hybrid with one of its parent species
invertebrate	An animal that does not have a backbone (vertebral column) or notochord
iwi	Maori word for tribe or tribes
kainga	Maori or Moriori village
kawenata	Term used for conservation covenants established on land owned by Maori/Moriori, with survey and fencing costs met by the Nga Whenui Rahui fund
koiwi	Human bones
krill	Shrimp-like marine animals eaten by baleen whales and seabirds
larva (*plural* larvae)	Distinctive juvenile stage of insect species that undergo complete metamorphosis to reach the adult stage, e.g. caterpillar (a moth or butterfly), grub (a beetle), or a maggot (fly)
leafroller	Caterpillar of the moth family Tortricidae, which lives inside a rolled or silk-tied leaf; also used as common name for the family
lignite	A brown biogenic sedimentary rock with woody texture, consisting of accumulated partially decomposed vegetation (low-grade coal)
limestone	A sedimentary rock formation that is made up of more than 50 per cent calcium carbonate; most limestone is of biogenic origin
liverwort	A member of a group of plants which, together with the mosses and hornworts, are known as Bryophytes. Liverworts are distinguished from mosses by the spores that are released from capsules that split along four longitudinal axes, rather than, as in mosses, opening at one end; and by root-like structures called rhizoids, which in liverworts are nearly always composed of a single elongated cell, but which in mosses are multicellular
macroalgae	Multicellular algae that are large enough to be seen with the naked eye

marae	A place to meet and debate issues in Maoridom; often a cluster of buildings including a meeting house (wharenui), or the open space in front of the wharenui, where formal greetings occur
megaherb	From 'mega' meaning large and 'herb' – any soft, non-woody plant. A term used mainly for large-leaved, non-woody subantarctic plants
Mesozoic	A major subdivision of geological time that includes the Triassic, Jurassic and Cretaceous Periods, spanning 135 million years from 200 to 65 million years ago
metamorphic rock	A rock that has been changed (recrystallised), in part or totally, as a function of pressure, heat and fluid activity; any pre-existing rock (igneous, sedimentary or metamorphic) can be metamorphosed
midden	An archaeological site attributed to human behaviour; normally a spoil heap of material or debris that has been deliberately discarded, such as shells associated with food preparation
Miocene	An 'epoch'; a formal subdivision of the Neogene Period of geological time, spanning 18.48 million years from 23.8 to 5.32 million years ago
monotypic genera	Genera that contain just the one species, e.g. Chatham Island sow thistle (*Embergeria grandifolia*) is the sole representative of the genus *Embergeria*
mollusc	Usually attributed to a shell; the Phylum Mollusca is a major group (phylum) of animals, most of which secrete a calcareous shell; it includes the bivalves, gastropods, scaphopods and cephalopods, including such well-known animals as scallops, snails and squid
muttonbirds	Large chicks of burrow-nesting petrels traditionally taken by Maori for human consumption; these days the word is mainly used to identify sooty shearwaters, both as a species and for the harvested chicks
naturalised	Introduced to a particular area directly or indirectly by human agency, and now established in the wild
obsidian	Naturally occurring volcanic glass, normally associated with silica-rich rhyolite volcanism
Oligocene	An 'epoch'; a formal subdivision of the Paleogene Period of geological time, spanning 9.9 million years from 33.7 to 23.8 million years ago
olivine basalt	A basalt with conspicuous crystals of the green mineral olivine
pa	Maori fortified village
palaeoecologist	Someone who specialises in ecological reconstructions on the basis of fossil evidence and environmental interpretation of the sediments or sedimentary rocks that the fossils relate to
Paleocene	An 'epoch'; a formal subdivision of the Paleogene Period of geological time, spanning 9.5 million years from 65.0 to 55.5 million years ago
Paleozoic	A major subdivision of geological time that includes the Cambrian, Ordovician, Silurian, Devonian, Carboniferous and Permian Periods, spanning 342 million years from 542 to 200 million years ago
pathogen	Any life-form that causes disease or ill-thrift in another
Permian	A 'period'; a formal subdivision of geological time spanning 48 million years from 299 to 251 million years ago

petiole	Stalk of a leaf
petroglyph	An archaeological feature; a carving in rock made by humans
phosphorite	A rock that is dominated by authigenic phosphate minerals
photosynthesis	The process by which plants (or rather bacteria trapped within their cells) convert solar energy into sugar
phylogeny	The study of the evolutionary relationships of plants and animals
Pleistocene	An 'epoch'; a formal subdivision of the Neogene Period of geological time, spanning 1.8 million years from 1.81 million years ago to 10,000 years ago
Pliocene	An 'epoch'; a formal subdivision of the Neogene Period of geological time, spanning 3.51 million years from 5.32 to 1.81 million years ago
podocarp	A major group of plants that arose in Paleozoic time, before the rise of the flowering plants in Mesozoic time; New Zealand examples include rimu, totara and matai
ponga	A tree fern; the term is often used for the trunk, especially when it is used for construction of a wall or shelter
propagate	To cause an organism to multiply or breed. A term often used exclusively for plants, whereby the intention is to produce further individuals using horticultural techniques
propagule	Any part of a plant or animal used for the purpose of propagation, i.e. to make more individuals, either by asexual or sexual means
pyroxene	A major group of common rock-forming minerals; black, magnesium-iron-calcium-aluminium silicate mineral ($(Ca,Mg,Fe)_2Si_2O_6$)
rakau momori	Traditional Moriori carvings on living kopi trees
redoubt	A fort, usually consisting of an enclosed defensive emplacement
rhizome	Underground stem of a plant
rhyolite	A silica-rich volcanic rock composed mainly of quartz, feldspar and volcanic glass; normally pale-coloured
saprobe	An organism that derives its nourishment from non-living or decaying organic matter
schist	A metamorphic rock with a pronounced planar structure, imparted by the common presence of flat minerals (especially mica)
scoria	Volcanic explosion debris, generally associated with basalt volcanoes, that accumulates near the crater and is usually highly vesicular (charged with gas bubbles)
sea mount	A submarine mountain or pinnacle rising from the sea floor, often volcanic in origin
sedimentary rock	A rock that is made up of sediment that has been deposited by a fluid, normally water or air; most sediment is derived from pre-existing rock material (gravel, sand, silt, mud) and biogenic material (remnant hard parts of plants and animals)
seismic activity	Relating to earthquakes; seismic energy behaves like waves
sessile	Sessile animals are attached to the substrate (typically the sea floor) and therefore unable to move about

siliceous	Dominated by silica or silicon dioxide (SiO_2)
silicified	Mineralised by silica or silicon dioxide (SiO_2)
strand	That portion of the shoreline where flotsam and jetsam such as driftwood, plastic bags and other rubbish are left stranded
subfossil	Bones of birds that have been dead for hundreds if not thousands of years, but have not yet become fossilised. Such remains occur abundantly in some dune and cave deposits on the Chatham Islands
subspecies	A subdivision of a species, usually considered capable of breeding with other subspecies of the same species, but typically isolated geographically
substratum/substrate	The surface on which organisms grow or are attached
subtidal	The zone of the marine environment that is permanently submerged, from the low-tide mark to the abyss
swamp	A wetland combining mineral and peat substrates, having moderate water flow, and typically of high fertility
sympatric	Referring to species (or taxa) that co-exist at the same site (opposite is 'allopatric')
tableland	A geological term used for land that is usually of moderately high relief, and whose summit slopes are flattened like a table. Tablelands are often caused by flood basalts, but may also be caused by extensive erosion
taxon (*plural* taxa)	A formally named biological entity, typically a species or subspecies
taxonomy	The study of the classification and naming of plants and animals
tectonic	Relating to tectonism, the processes that deform the Earth's crust and cause it to change shape
temperate	The term describing those latitudes lying between the subtropics and the subantarctic (in the Southern Hemisphere) or subarctic (Northern Hemisphere); typically the climate has summer and winters that are mild, rather than extremely hot or cold
tephra	Solid particulate product of volcanic eruption; normally airborne; commonly referred to as 'volcanic ash'
test (zoology)	The hard calcareous shell of sea urchins and other echinoderms
tikanga	Correct procedure or custom (Maori or Moriori)
topographical surface	A surface developed on land
topography	The shape of a surface; normally attributed to the land surface or sea floor
trachyandesite	A particular type of volcanic rock with a silica content higher than a basalt, approaching that of an andesite, and containing alkali feldspar
trachyte	A particular type of volcanic rock derived from basalt, containing alkali feldspar
translocation	The deliberate transfer of a species to a new site, these days usually done to improve conservation status
Triassic	A 'period'; a formal subdivision of geological time spanning 51 million years from 251 to 200 million years ago

tsunami	A major disturbance within a water mass, normally the sea or ocean, with very large wave-length (kilometres to tens of kilometres); commonly triggered by fault displacement of the sea floor in association with major earthquakes
tuff	A distinctive rock type formed from volcanic ash or tephra
turangawaewae	A Maori word referring to the place where a person has the right to live, typically through ancestral connection
turf vegetation	Low vegetation (usually less than 3cm tall) forming a dense carpet
vascular plants	Plants with conducting tissues (mainly ferns, conifers and flowering plants), contrasting with non-vascular plants (e.g. mosses and algae)
vertebrae	Individual bones that collectively form a backbone (vertebral column or spine)
vertebrate	An animal that has a backbone (vertebral column) or notochord
whitebait	Edible larvae or juveniles of many herring-like fishes; in New Zealand the juveniles of several species of *Galaxias* that are caught in river mouths as they migrate back into rivers from their larval development in coastal waters. The main whitebait species on the Chatham Islands is the common smelt (*Retropinna retropinna*)
Zealandia	The largely submergent tract of continental crust that broke away from Gondwanaland 83 million years ago; about half the size of Australia; New Zealand and New Caledonia are the largest emergent areas (about 7 per cent) within Zealandia

INDEX

(Including glossary of scientific names)

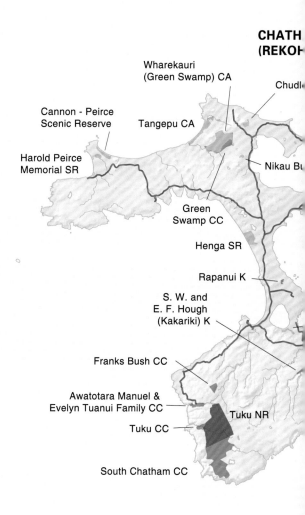

THE SISTERS
(RANGITATAHI)

CHATH
(REKOH

Wharekauri
(Green Swamp) CA

Chudl

Cannon - Peirce
Scenic Reserve

Tangepu CA

Harold Peirce
Memorial SR

Nikau Bu

Green
Swamp CC

Henga SR

Rapanui K

S. W. and
E. F. Hough
(Kakariki) K

Franks Bush CC

Awatotara Manuel &
Evelyn Tuanui Family CC

Tuku NR

Tuku CC

South Chatham CC

Public land

NR		Nature Reserve
NHR		National Historic Reserve
HR		Historic Reserve
SR		Scenic Reserve
CA		Conservation Area

Private land

CC		Conservation Covenant
K		Kawenata

Only protected areas larger than 30 hectares are shown

E CHATHAM ISLANDS

-N-

URI)

Mail   Point Munning CC

Kaingaroa Station CC

M Barker (Hapupu) NHR

Farm HR

Bush HR

atea SR

FORTY FOURS
(MOTUHARA)

pie Creek CC

a East K

a K

PITT ISLAND
(RANGIAURIA)

eehan CC   STAR KEYS
                           (MOTUHOPE)
          Tupuangi

NR   Frederick and Mary
                  Hunt Memorial CC

aipaua SR   Ellen Elizabeth Preece
                  (Caravan Bush) CC
auria SR

r Cove SR   Rangatira
                  (South East Island) NR

HE PYRAMID   0   25 km
TARAKOIKOIA)